EXPLORING LANGUAGE

Peter Doughty
John Pearce
Geoffrey Thornton

Schools Council Programme in
Linguistics and English Teaching

EDWARD ARNOLD

TO
M.A.K.H.

Other publications in the Programme
Language in Use
Language in Use Tape

Printed in Great Britain by
Western Printing Services Ltd, Bristol

Contents

Foreword

Language intervenes between man and
nature acting upon him internally and externally
William von Humboldt

This book is written for teachers, and those training to become teachers, because the authors believe that it is part of every teacher's job to think about the part played by language in teaching and learning. It is not an analysis of English grammar, nor an introduction to Linguistic Science, nor a text-book on how to study language in the class-room, but an account of how human beings 'use language to live'. Its point of departure is the individual's own understanding of the nature and function of language which he has acquired in the process of learning a language, and it proceeds by asking him to review this understanding in the light of an objectively linguistic approach to language. Its aim is to convince a reader that understanding language is important to anyone involved in teaching and learning; and that exploring language need be neither arid nor technically formidable for the layman.

Each chapter of the book opens up a key area in the exploration of language, but the limitations of space have meant that many important topics have had to be dealt with very briefly. The idea is to show a reader what is important for the study of language from the point of view of teaching and learning. To discover more, he will have to go on to the literature of Linguistic Studies, and to help him each chapter ends with a number of suggestions for further reading.

The growth of *Exploring Language* has been closely associated with the growth of *Language in Use*, the new approach to the teaching of English language developed by the same authors. *Language in Use* represents the practical implementation of the idea of exploring language. It is written for the teacher and enables him to take up a linguistic approach to language with secondary school pupils, and

5

college students, of all types and conditions. Although developed for the teacher of English, its form is such that any teacher would be able to use it if he wanted to see what the argument of *Exploring Language* could lead to with his own pupils in the class-room. To help the teacher who wants to do this, there is an appendix included which relates the chapters of *Exploring Language* to the units of *Language in Use*.

In conclusion, I wish to thank all those people who have helped us with the writing of this book. First and foremost, Professor M. A. K. Halliday has been a continuous source of encouragement to the authors and an invaluable stimulus to hard thinking. We have also had the benefit of many discussions with Professor Basil Bernstein and Professor Mary Douglas, both of whom have contributed so much to the underlying thinking behind the argument of the book. Finally, there are the many people in schools and colleges who have seen various parts of the book at different stages in its development. We are very clear that a book of this kind develops best out of vigorous and wide-ranging discussion, such as they were willing to engage in with us.

Peter Doughty

University College London
July 1971

One   Language, teaching and learning

1

There is no more difficult subject to write about than language. Everyone possesses well-developed thoughts and feelings about it, because these are a normal accompaniment to learning a language. Moreover, someone who reads a book like this is likely to have a more than usually well-developed set of attitudes to language and its use, because he will have undergone a long process of formal education, and formal education has a very strong influence upon these attitudes. If the book is not only about language, but also about the part played by language in learning and teaching, the position is still more complicated, because its most likely readers will then be teachers or those training to be teachers, and, of all people, teachers are likely to have very strong views about language and its use. Their experience of formal education includes college as well as school as a source of ideas about language, and their subsequent professional experience adds to them the preoccupation of the teacher with the use of language for learning. They are likely, therefore, to point out that their view of the nature and function of language is already well developed and that they cannot really see the professional value to them of enquiring into it.

While at times their ideas about language certainly provide teachers with a true insight, at others they can be very misleading, or even quite untrue, when tested against an objectively linguistic view of language. When so much professional discussion of teaching focuses upon subject matter, and most discussion of how to teach focuses upon method, it is easy to overlook the fact that language is, and must be, the major medium for both teaching and learning. In order to show that there is a great deal to be said about language in teaching and learning, it is necessary to look first at the origin and nature of those ideas that form the basis of most teachers' thoughts about language.

The process of learning our own language is an inseparable part of growing up as a normal human being. This process of learning, however, involves not only familiar things like the grammar and vocabulary of our native language, or mother tongue, but much less familiar things like our understanding of what we can use

7

language for and what it will do for us. As Geoffrey Thornton points out in Chapter 3, part of what a child learns about language is that he can use language to get things done, or to affect the behaviour of other members of his family. In the same way, the young adolescent will have to learn how to use language for initiating and maintaining relationships, especially with members of the opposite sex. The young teacher has to learn how to use language for exercising control over others in the context of his own class-room. The experienced teacher, elevated to the position of Head of Department, of Deputy-Head, or Headmaster, is faced with the task of learning how to use language for maintaining appropriately professional relationships with the rest of the Staff. Such learning as this already goes well beyond the mere question of acquiring grammar and vocabulary.

At each stage in an individual's learning of his language, however, there is something learnt in addition both to the basic forms, or patterns, of the language, and the knowledge of how to use them in a given situation. Along with them come attitudes to both the patterns and to how they should be used. These attitudes colour our own use of language and our response to the way in which others use it. For example, people hold very strong ideas about the rightness or wrongness, pleasantness or ugliness, of the sounds others make in speaking the language. People also possess very clear ideas about what ways of using the language are appropriate to what contexts. If challenged about their views, and asked to justify them, or say where they acquired them, people appeal to what is 'obvious', 'self-evident', 'natural', 'clear to any thinking man', or will show complete surprise that any justification can be asked for, or is at all practicable. This is because views about the nature and function of language, like language itself, are learnt intuitively, and therefore do not seem open to review or discussion. There is a common sense view of the world that we live in which is sometimes referred to as a 'folk-wisdom' and which provides a similarly intuitive understanding of people and their behaviour. Our native speaker's intuitions about language and how men use it can thus be referred to as a 'folk linguistic', a 'common sense' about the language we live by.

An important part of people's folk linguistic comes from their experience at school. It is a product of what they are actually told about language and how they see its forms and uses valued by those who teach them and by the pattern of syllabus, curriculum and examination that they work through. The commonest idea most people derive from this source is that somehow writing is the 'proper' form of the language and speaking somehow a debased or imperfect or slipshod version of it. For teachers, the experience of college is added to that of school, and then the everyday working environment of the school itself, so that most teachers come to have a particularly well-developed folk linguistic, especially insofar as it embraces common sense ideas about pupils' use of language and learning. For this reason, the teacher is likely to be sceptical about the value of discussing the part played by language in his work. It is not at all clear to him that there is anything to be said on the subject which could relate to his needs and problems as a teacher. As one teacher in a college of education put it, 'Language has nothing to do with the teaching of Geography,' and a lecturer in the English department of a new University went so far as to say that 'Language cannot *be* discussed. It is itself.' In both cases, there was the sincere conviction that the job of teacher did not require a professional concern with the nature and function of language, or the part it plays in learning.

2

The central purpose of this book is to demonstrate that language *can* be a fascinating and profitable subject for discussion, and that this discussion can be made to bear directly upon the professional problems and concerns of all teachers. It asks the reader to re-examine something with which he is already intimately familiar. It makes the assumption that the reader is, by definition, a competent and experienced user of a native language, or mother tongue, so that he does possess a well-developed intuitive understanding of the nature and function of language. He brings this understanding to his reading of the book, and the book proceeds by asking him to become much more consciously aware of the ideas and assumptions that that understanding embraces. Its aim is not so much to tell him things that he does not know as to sharpen and make much more explicit the things that he does know but has not perhaps reflected upon with sufficient objectivity for his professional needs.

In discussing people's knowledge of the nature and function of

9

society that they acquire merely by being members of a society, the American sociologist, Peter Berger, suggests that exploring society will not provide:

> ". . . the excitement of coming upon the totally unfamiliar, but rather the excitement of finding the familiar becoming transformed in its meaning.'

The language that we speak is as familiar to us as the society in which we live and our intuitive understanding of language is closely parallel to our intuitive understanding of our experience as members of a family, a community, or a society. In both cases, to go beyond this intuitive understanding it is necessary to distance ourselves from the subject in question in order to overcome the sense that it is all so obvious and everyday a part of living that any exploration must be unprofitable, or even undesirable. At the same time, it would be foolish to set aside this intuitive understanding as though the experience of living in society or speaking a language was in some sense irrelevant to finding out more about them. This is why Berger's idea, that what needs to happen is a transformation of the familiar, is so important for this book. Ideally, at the end of each chapter a reader should find himself saying 'how true', rather than 'how extraordinary'; 'I never thought of it that way', rather than 'Who would have thought it would be like that?'

Transforming what is familiar, however, is not merely a process of making oneself consciously aware of those things that before were only known intuitively. It also involves a process of review, for, while our folk-linguistic contains much that accords with a rational and objective view of language and its use, it also contains many things that do not. A competent speaker will vary his form of words according to the situation in which he finds himself; and he is well aware that a key factor in determining his choice of words will be the other people present, and his relationship to them. An objective view of language in use will confirm his intuitions by pointing to the variety of ways of speaking that occur in all languages, and the degree to which this can be related in a rational and orderly fashion to the variety of situations in which people meet face-to-face. On the other hand, folk-linguistic views of variations in accent present a different case. People's intuitive understanding here leads them to put a particular value on some accents rather than on others, and to attribute to the sound patterns of the language themselves aesthetic judge-

10

ments that lie in the ear, or the social consciousness, of the hearer. An objective view of the matter will say that variation in the sound patterns of language is as much a natural feature of language as variation which arises from speaking. The variations in the sound patterns of a language that are commonly referred to as 'accent' do not affect the intrinsic capacity of the language to convey meaning. Only those unfamiliar with a particular accent are likely to find difficulty in understanding those who speak it. In this sense, one accent is as linguistically good as another as a way of using the sound patterns of the language. Whether or not one accent is as widely usable as another is a social rather than a linguistic question. Therefore judgements about their suitability in a given context, or their quality as sound, are social or aesthetic judgements and are not acceptable as assessments of inadequacies which are supposed to be a part of language itself.

These two examples illustrate an important difference in the potential effect of exploring language upon a reader's folk-linguistic. By asking him to focus upon the diversity of language, the range of varieties that he uses, both spoken and written, and the subtlety with which they are intuitively selected to fit the appropriate context, exploring language can make him more consciously aware of something that is already familiar to him. In this sense, its effect is to confirm his existing intuitions about it, and its value lies in its power to bring about a new awareness of their validity. An exploration of variety in speech, however, shows that folk-linguistic understanding of accent does not necessarily accord with an objective view of the facts. A reader may well come to realise in this way that his own intuitions express as much a personal or social judgement of people as a linguistic understanding of language, and that his own folk-linguistic does not necessarily represent the truth about language and its use. It is as if the furniture of a familiar room were not only to rearrange itself before our eyes, but proceed to transform itself into chairs and tables and cupboards of a design quite unlike anything we have seen before, or would be likely to choose if we had. It is as though the original room represents the world as we have always understood it to be, and to have reality transformed in front of our eyes can be most unsettling.

Exploring language from an objectively linguistic point of view is capable of producing a 'transformation' in the understanding of

11

language, because it enables an individual to re-examine his view of linguistic reality. It helps him to focus attention upon aspects of that reality which are regularly overlooked, like the relationship between the categories of a language and its speaker's interpretation of the world, and it enables him to go beyond the limiting understanding of folk-linguistic. Unmodified, folk-linguistic can lead a speaker to distort linguistic events through over-simplifying them, as with the process of language acquisition; misinterpreting them, as with the nature of fluent speech; or actually misrepresenting them, as with the view that the study of language is essentially a study of 'words'. In most instances, therefore, the process of exploring language reveals that things are not quite what they seem. Berger suggests that the parallel everyday ideas about the workings of society can be subjected to the same sort of exploration with the result that:

> 'Social reality turns out to have many layers of meaning. The discovery of each new layer changes the perception of the whole.'

Folk-linguistic leads people to believe that *linguistic* reality can have only one layer of meaning, but the reader is invited to discover that it possesses many layers of meaning. Discovering new layers of meaning in familiar ideas about language is likely to change his whole perception of its nature and function.

The idea of linguistic reality plays an important part in all the chapters that follow. It is a convenient way of referring to an individual's cumulative experience of languaging taken in its broadest and most general sense. If the subject of this book were the physical world, its multiplicity of structures and patterns and the forces by which it is ordered, then it would be possible to call an individual's cumulative experience of shape and colour, temperature and pressure and movement, his understanding of 'physical reality'. If the subject were literature, then the sum of all that a reader has added to his understanding through his reading of fictions, be they novels, poetry or plays, goes to make up his experience of 'literary reality'. This naturally embraces any effect his reading of fictions has had in widening or deepening, and thereby modifying his interpretation of the world and his judgement of men and things. Similarly, an individual's cumulative experience of language and its use, acquired by learning it and using it as an ordinary member of a human community, goes to make up his understanding of linguistic reality. It

12

embraces his power to use his knowledge of language to interpret his experience of the world and to form relationships with others.

Linguistic reality makes its presence felt in day-to-day living through the thoughts and feelings and assumptions which go to make up folk-linguistic. If a speaker uses a common phrase like 'I don't call that good English', or 'She speaks so nicely', or 'Don't use that expression, it's rude', or 'You must learn to write in paragraphs', or simply writes the word 'Spelling!' on the bottom of a piece of work, he is necessarily expressing a view of an aspect of linguistic reality. Similarly, attitudes to accent and to the relationship of language to the context in which it occurs are part of an individual's view of linguistic reality. There is an important difference, however, between these two instances. In the case of the relationship between language and its context, our view of linguistic reality will normally be confirmed by an objectively linguistic view of the matter. A similar view of the nature and variety of the sound patterns of a language, however, is almost certain to contradict any previously held folk-linguistic view of the matter. In this case, the likely effect of exploring language is to suggest major modifications in an individual's view of linguistic reality. Where a folk-linguistic view of language and its use does not accord with an objectively linguistic view, the aim of *Exploring Language* is therefore to 'transform the familiar' by bringing about a reinterpretation of linguistic reality.

3

So far, the question of exploring language has been discussed without considering the special position of the teacher. While an understanding of the nature and function of language could interest him in its own right, his particular concern will be to see in what sense this understanding can be relevant to the context of the class-room and the needs of his pupils. Yet even in so plain a statement of the case as this, there is a problem, for who is a teacher, what is meant by a class-room, and what is a 'pupil'?

As far as exploring language is concerned, anyone who has a teaching responsibility is a teacher, be it in an infant, junior, middle-secondary, comprehensive, approved, or special school; in colleges of education, further education, technology, art or business; or in university work of all kinds. Whatever the label on the institution, or its particular demands and problems, those teaching in it use the same medium, language, and correspondingly have the same need to understand the part it plays in teaching and learning. In the same way, 'class-room' has to include all those situations where pupils are gathered together for the purpose of learning. The word itself, however, is so closely tied to the school context in the minds of most people that the term 'learning situation' better suits the wide scope of language enquiry. Moreover, it underlies the fact that such situations are called in to being in order to make learning possible rather than to provide occasions for teaching. It has the added advantage that it can also cover less formal situations like group discussion, seminar, or face-to-face tutorial.

It would be convenient if there were as readily available a term to cover all those who participate as learners in learning situations, but it is a significant cultural fact about our use of language that we do not have a commonly used word for the purpose. The one word that is available, 'learner', has been effectively restricted by common usage to imply 'someone who is beginning to master a skill' as in 'learner-driver'. All the other possible words, like child, pupil, or student, have built into their use assumptions about age, or ability, or status that make it difficult to use them to refer to something as general as 'participant in a learning situation'. They illustrate beautifully the ordering of experience, built into the very words of the language, that is explored in Chapter 4. The fact that the word 'child' implies 'one who is wholly dependent upon an adult for guidance' and 'one who has no rights as an individual human being by virtue of that dependence' is often overlooked by those who use it so freely to refer to pupils in secondary schools. Similarly, part of the difference in meaning between 'pupil' and 'student' is that a pupil is 'one who is taught', while a student is 'one who learns'. In the minds of many people, a pupil is also 'one who remains ignorant, unless he is taught the facts', while a student is 'one who can learn for himself'. Given the particular nature of enquiry into language, the word 'student' seemed better suited to this book than 'pupil' as the term for 'any participant in a learning situation'. It seemed less ridiculous to imply thereby that 5-year-olds in the infant class were 'students' than to impose the common meanings of 'pupil' upon all those who might find themselves enquiring into language.

So, the focus of this book is upon learning situations, and the degree

14

to which teachers' and students' use of language for learning determines their character and effectiveness. Once more, however, a plain statement of the case conceals a difficulty. The reader will have assumed that 'learning situation' necessarily implies some formal educational framework such as a school or a college, or the structure of a course provides. Many of the things about language that require special notice in this context, however, apply also to the much less formally organised situations which occur in the ordinary course of doing a job.

The work-bench, or the city office, or the construction site create innumerable situations in which doing the job includes learning how to do it. In these situations, just as in the class-room or lecture theatre, effective participation depends upon the learner's ability to come to terms with the language being used by the individual doing the teaching. True though this may be, it is still necessary to be able to distinguish between learning situations whose aim is purely educational and those that occur as part of some other activity. This book therefore talks about formal, as opposed to informal, learning situations when the context is specifically school or college or a planned and structured course.

A further complication arises out of the fact that all learning situations, formal and informal, combine two distinct types of learning. There is the subject or topic or task that is the focus of the situation, a curriculum component like French or physics or writing computer programmes, or a seminar topic like audio-visual methods, or a work-task like operating a turret-lathe or driving a fork-lift truck. Then there is the language through which the learning takes place. A class who are trying to orient maps, or carry out the dissection of an earthworm, for the first time, are in the process of adding to their existing knowledge of geography or biology, but they are also extending their knowledge of language at the same time. This topic forms the subject of Chapter 7, so that here it is only necessary to point out that learning situations entail some measure of language learning, however small. Successful learning for those taking part will depend upon their being able to come to terms with both the subject matter *and* the language for learning that the situation demands.

It may seem surprising to suggest that there could be a single factor of this kind which enters into all situations. Our advanced industrial

15

society has grown so bewilderingly complex, and contains such an enormous diversity of activities, that it is often very difficult to see the similarities between things. It is made more difficult because the differences are usually easily visible on the surface of things, in the dress that people wear, the machines that they work with, the buildings in which they work. Moreover, the common language in which we refer to them emphasises the differences, because it is primarily through language that they are registered. We talk about infants, juniors, backward children, average pupils, sixth-formers, students, and undergraduates, and focus upon any one of these types of learner as if it shared no common features with any of the others. As the argument of this chapter has so far suggested, however, it is possible to look for those things which everyone in a learning situation shares in common with everyone else. One of these is the fact that they have to draw upon the resources of the language at some stage in order that learning can, in fact, take place. Another is that the process of drawing upon the resources of the language is likely to involve an element of language learning, what is described in Chapter 7 as a minimum growth of competence. A third, the most important of all, is that everyone has to use the same basic processes of the brain in coping with these linguistic demands.

4

The special position of the teacher, however, is that he must necessarily make very heavy demands upon his students' competence, in particular upon their ability to use language specifically for the processes of formal learning. A common way of regarding any formal learning situation is to see it as a situation in which the ignorance of the student is to be modified by his acquisition of new knowledge. It is the teacher's task to present what is new and the student's to show that he has mastered what has been presented. As customarily practised, both these processes involve a particular way of drawing upon the resources of the language. At various points in the book the authors make use of Professor Halliday's idea that the process of languaging involves a number of different ways of looking at the function of language. He suggests that part of the business of learning language is to learn what language can be used for. A young child comes to realise that language causes things to happen; that it can be used by others to exercise control over him; and that his relationship to others is 'largely mediated through language'. As he grows up, so his experience of what language can be used for forms in his mind a number of models of how language functions. It is as though he ends with a number of test cards that he can use to assess what is and is not a possible way of languaging. We usually remain quite unaware of these models, for they only exist independently of each other for a very short period of time during the initial stage of language learning before a child is two. They form an essential part of our view of linguistic reality, however, because they determine what we believe we can do with language. The deep unease many people feel when faced with certain uses of language, such as highly abstract rational argument or densely metaphoric imaginative prose, may be a sign that they do not 'understand', in the conventional sense of the word, but it may also be a sign that language is being used in such a way that its very purpose, its function, escapes them. There is nothing in their own apprehension of linguistic reality to which they can relate it.

This situation can very easily arise in the context of formal learning, because a teacher is often unaware that his own use of language, and his expectations about the kind of language which he wants to see his students using, are both dominated by one particular model out of a possible seven that Professor Halliday distinguishes (see p. 46). This is the REPRESENTATIONAL model, language 'as . . . a means of communicating about something, of expressing propositions'. It is the use of language to convey an informational message; to make explicit and ordered reference to objects and processes; or to construct an argument, so ordered that each element in it bears a proper and discernible relationship to the rest. It is the language of the 'essay', the 'notes', the 'write-up', and the 'report': the language of the subject text-book and the public examination.

Language for learning in the context of our subject-based curriculum, is often taken to be virtually synonymous with REPRESENTATIONAL language. In consequence, this model dominates the professional folk-linguistic of most teachers. They are accustomed to judge the value of any use of language against their conception of representational language. Its influence permeates the terms in which they habitually discuss the linguistic aspects of their student's work. It is present in the idea that all language appropriate to formal learning should be *accurate* and *logical*; and that a minimum requirement for effective work in the context of formal learning is

17

a command of a *reasonable* and *grammatical* written English. Its fullest expression lies in the widely held belief that there is one ideal form of 'good English' in which the virtues of simplicity, clarity, rationality, and urbanity are combined; and that this alone is the appropriate linguistic medium for formal learning. Moreover, it is commonly believed that the ability to use language of this kind is a proper test of whether or not a student has 'ability'. His competence in handling representational language is equated with his over-all 'intelligence'. This one model's dominant place in a teacher's view of linguistic reality may thus end up by influencing his entire approach to his students' capabilities as learners.

The unique responsibility of the teacher is that he is in a position to dictate the linguistic terms within which learning is allowed to take place. If he sees a particular type of language, or pattern of usage, as the only one that is appropriate to his work, then his students can only satisfy him by using it effectively. The student, however, has only one source from which he can derive the language for learning that he knows is expected of him, the teacher himself. Consequently, the teacher's own use of language comes to play a critically important part in the pupil's ability to learn. His attitude to language also affects their attitude to learning itself. In spite of all that has happened to modify the old rigid boundaries between subjects, it is still the case that students are reluctant to deploy in one area of the curriculum what they have acquired in another. Students fail to distinguish between the facts and the way that they have learnt to language them in the context of a particular area of the curriculum. They identify what they learn with the linguistic forms in which they learnt it, so that what is done in Geography or Biology or English does not seem to be usable in any other context. If a teacher insists that a particular task must be carried out by using a particular form of words, then the student is likely to end up by believing that he is only capable of carrying it out successfully insofar as he can use the same form of words. This intimate relationship between the teacher's view of language for learning and the student's understanding of what it is to learn underlies the basic argument of this book that educational success is so often primarily a matter of linguistic success. Before a failure to learn can be attributed to a lack of conceptual 'ability', it must be shown that it is not a consequence of failure to language appropriately according to the preconceived notions of the teacher concerned.

18

An understanding of the nature and function of language is thus quite central to the practical professional concerns of any teacher. Both he and his students acquire language as ordinary human beings, and both develop a view of linguistic reality that expresses itself through their folk-linguistic. Met together in a formal learning situation, they must use language for the processes of teaching and learning, and they bring to this situation their cumulative experience as users of a mother tongue. Their experience of language as individuals and as members of society is a basic factor in the situation. Because it is a formal learning situation, their previous experience of language for learning is particularly important. It determines what ways of using language they believe acceptable for learning, in the broad sense, and what particular pattern of usage they believe appropriate to any particular task that confronts them.

The teacher has come to give so dominant a place to the representational model in his professional view of linguistic reality, that he is not aware of the other functions to anything like the same degree. In the context of formal learning, moreover, he considers that this model defines the only acceptable way of using language for learning. However, his students tend to carry into the class-room a much stronger awareness that language is for doing many things other than languaging propositionally. Hence, there is so often a wide difference between teachers' and students' views of linguistic reality, when they meet in a formal learning situation. Moreover, the model of language that looms largest in the teacher's view of linguistic reality insofar as it touches formal learning seems to figure least strongly in the average students' intuitions about the nature and function of language. In effect, the dominance of the representational model over his habitual view of language for learning leads the teacher to create a situation in which the language he wants is a form of language that comes least readily to the majority of those he teaches.

In this situation, it is particularly important that the teacher is fully aware of what is going on. He needs to be able to see how his pupils came by their language and what factors influenced its acquisition. He needs to be able to review his own experience as a language learner and user, and he must be able to relate the linguistic activity within the context of formal learning to what can be said about the

19

nature and function of language as such. This, finally, is the argument for insisting that the exploration of language has a place in the professional thinking of all teachers.

FURTHER READING

P. L. Berger, *Invitation to Sociology* (Penguin).

P. L. Berger and T. Luckmann, *The Social Construction of Reality* (Penguin).

P. S. Doughty, *Language in English*, in Papers in Linguistics and English Teaching, Series II (Longman).

P. S. Doughty, *English in the curriculum*, in Papers in Linguistics and English Teaching, Series II (Longman).

P. S. Doughty, *An Introduction to Linguistics for the teacher of English*, in Nuffield Papers in Linguistics and English Teaching (Longman).

M. A. K. Halliday, 'Language and Experience' in *The Place of Language* (Educational Review, Vol. 20, No. 2, 1968).

Two   Understanding, exploration and awareness

1

When something enters into every aspect of our lives in the way that language does, its very familiarity is a barrier to exploration. Existing understanding will always seem sufficient, and exploration merely a process of elaborating an abstruse disguise for what is commonplace and familiar. The crucial part played by language in formal learning, however, really asks of the teacher something more than an unmodified folk-linguistic understanding of language. Insofar as language is the critical factor in the success of teaching and learning, an objectively linguistic 'awareness' of its nature and function is essential to the professional needs of every teacher. This chapter discusses the different kinds of understanding of language that we possess and shows how the idea of exploring language can fit into the general pattern of what people know about language. In particular, it shows how exploring language is related to the scientific study of language.

Initially, it is necessary to distinguish between knowledge OF a language and knowledge ABOUT language. Knowledge of a language derives solely from the process of learning language, while knowledge about language embraces the intuitions of folk-linguistic and all kinds of knowledge about language that are conscious and explicit. Knowledge OF language is something that every reader of this book possesses. Moreover, it is knowledge that every human being possesses unless there has been some kind of brain damage to prevent its acquisition. Chapter 3 describes how children are born with a capacity to acquire language, just as they are born with a capacity to discriminate sounds or to see three-dimensionally. This capacity, however, is no more than an innate disposition to process the patterns of natural language. Language itself is the product of using this capacity in a specific human context. The patterns that the child acquires depend, of course, upon the particular speech community into which he is born; hence an individual's 'knowledge of a language' amounts to his ability to use a mother tongue.

This knowledge is what is implied by the linguist's reference to the 'competent speaker/hearer'. In this context, 'competent' means only that a speaker is able to make use of a natural language for all the normal purposes of living as a member of a particular speech community. Needless to say, an individual who is in this sense a 'competent speaker/hearer' is not, necessarily, one who can also cope successfully with any language situation he might meet in as complex a society as ours. The term 'speaker/hearer' emphasises the fact that language is primarily a matter of speech and that the most representative of all ways of using language is the situation in which two or three people talk to each other, face-to-face. Each speaks and is spoken to; each listens and is heard.

A competent speaker/hearer, then, possesses 'knowledge of a language', and this is the basis of his 'competence' to meet the linguistic demands of living and learning. It is the knowledge that is needed for the exercise of command of a language. (The question of competence and command of a language is dealt with in Chapter 7.) In the process of becoming a competent speaker/hearer, however, an individual does not only acquire the patterns of a language. He develops along with them, a body of intuitions about their proper use. Professor Halliday's 'models of language' discriminate a number of linguistic functions that underlie the way in which a language is actually used by its speakers. The individual's knowledge of the things he can do with his language that these models describe make up an essential part of his total knowledge of his language. The child who says 'I want Teddy', because he knows that Teddy is likely to appear if he speaks those words, has learnt to put together meaningfully a selection from the phonological, grammatical, and lexical patterns of his language. At the same time, he has also developed the intuition that one use for language is to get things done, or to cause them to happen when you want them to happen. When a voice says "Don't do it again, or you'll go to bed", and he has learnt to connect the patterns of this utterance with the swift appearance of bed if he does do it again, he has developed an intuition that language can be used to exercise control over him. This kind of intuitive knowledge of language is then a knowledge of language function, a prerequisite for using language appropriately and thus an essential element in the knowledge of a language that goes to make up the competence of the competent speaker/hearer.

'Intuitions', however, can refer to two distinct ways of knowing. Both affect us in such a way that their presence as a factor in languaging remains largely unconscious. Intuitions that develop as part

22

of our knowledge of a language are *functional*, because they form an integral part of the business of using language to live. Folk-linguistic intuitions, however, are used to *interpret* cultural experience of language. When faced with a person's accent, or his choice of words in a letter, we judge, or assess, how we react to them. This reaction is often expressed in terms of an implied standard. Accents are 'poor', or 'refined', or 'unintelligible', or 'rich'; words are 'too formal', 'mere jargon', 'beautifully expressive', or 'imaginatively handled'. Although they do operate for the most part unconsciously, folk-linguistic intuitions, therefore, are best seen as knowledge ABOUT, rather than knowledge OF language.

Like language, the ability to walk upright is a characteristically human activity, the product of an innate potential, genetically programmed, and a process of learning. Like language, again, one consequence of that process of learning is the acquisition of intuitions about the potentialities and limits of being able to balance, walk, run, climb, and so on. Such intuitions about walking or running are quite distinct from knowing what actions legs and arms and trunk have to perform in order to do these things. When we run, we show we understand what running can be used for, and the limits that physique and fitness impose upon our actions. This understanding amounts to a functional intuition about the physical possibilities of human locomotion. In contrast, each individual also possesses an understanding of who should and who should not run where and when, in his culture. Some people would not run in a church, or in a business suit, or in a skirt. Some men think it improper for women to run, while others take running about in the street as a sign that children are out of control. Most people assume that adults walk if they can, therefore an adult seen running requires a particular interpretation like "Stop, thief", or "Train to catch". For many people running because one felt full of the joys of spring would seem impossible if one were over twenty. These various attitudes and assumptions about running are interpretative rather than functional and a product of growing up and living in a particular culture. Hence they correspond to the kind of attitudes and assumptions about language that make up a folk-linguistic.

2

This distinction between functional intuitions that are part of a competent speaker's knowledge OF his language, and interpretative intuitions that properly belong to his knowledge ABOUT language, reveals the need for a further distinction between two kinds of knowledge about language. There is a 'knowledge about' that is acquired through the process of learning and using a language, the product of cultural learning; and there is an explicit 'knowledge about' that is gained primarily through the education system as a consequence of being taught English or a foreign language.

While folk-linguistic assumptions normally work unconsciously, it is possible to become *consciously* aware of them in particular circumstances. Responses to other people's accents are likely to be a quite unconscious expression of folk-linguistic. We do not normally give thought to our assessment of what sound patterns of English strike us as admirable and acceptable, and what we reject as ugly and unacceptable. If, however, a son or daughter uses a pattern that *is* unacceptable to us, we may well find ourselves articulating a 'theory of good speech' in order to give expression to our disapproval. A phrase such as "Don't ever say that word again", or "Must you use jargon?", expresses response to some word or phrase that does not match the speaker's intuitive awareness of what seems acceptable and what does not. If, however, reasons are demanded, an individual focuses consciously on what has been said and draws from his folk-linguistic a 'theory of good usage'. He might suggest that 'bloody idiot' is not an appropriate form of address between members of a family, or that it is not necessary to talk about 'signal to noise ratio' in discussing adequate reception on cheap transistor radios.

Even though a speaker can make himself aware of his folk-linguistic assumptions in this way, explicit and deliberate attention to the nature and function of language forms very little part of the process. Knowledge ABOUT that forms part of a folk-linguistic does not help a speaker to distance himself from his experience of language. Unless he can stand back from this experience, language remains too inextricably a part of his familiar world for its exploration to be possible. Knowledge OF language gives a speaker his functional understanding of language and his folk-linguistic gives him a cultural understanding of language, but neither of these, unaided, can provide him with an understanding of language that is objective. We would not expect that the ability to interpret space three-

24

dimensionally would yield, unaided, knowledge about the laws of perspective; nor would we expect that the ability to walk would itself yield knowledge about the muscles of the leg. In order to go further, some form of deliberate exploration of language is needed.

The teacher, therefore, needs to be able to explore language in such a way that he will be able to stand outside his own experience of language and look again at its nature and function. The understanding of language that comes from being a competent speaker/hearer and a member of a culture must, however, provide the point of departure. He needs to see the familiar and the obvious about language from an objective linguistic point of view, yet it is important that the familiar and the obvious remain recognisable in the process. Exploring language is such a form of enquiry. It enables the teacher to distance himself from his own experience of language in order to take an objectively linguistic view, while, at the same time, allowing him to retain that experience as a continuously relevant point of reference for his findings.

So far, this chapter has been focused upon the broad distinction between knowledge OF language and intuitive knowledge ABOUT language. For most people, a very large part of their activities as users of language is determined solely by these two kinds of knowledge. It is now time to consider, however, the distinction between a speaker's intuitive knowledge whether OF or ABOUT, and what he consciously and readily recognises as 'knowledge' about language. The school curriculum normally provides two sources of this kind of knowledge: learning a foreign language and what is usually time-tabled or examined as 'English Language'. When an individual refers to this kind of knowledge, or makes use of it, he recognises that he *is* using knowledge about language, for it corresponds to what he understands by the word in its everyday sense.

At some stage most people have had to learn a characteristic set of facts about language like irregular verbs in French or word order in German. 'Clause' and 'sentence', the word 'grammar' itself, are known from the definitions that were given in 'English Language' lessons. As the source of these facts is the class-room, people remain very aware of their status as 'knowledge' when using them. They are classified as 'facts', because they are like anything else learnt in the class-rooms. Thus, the most common explicit knowledge ABOUT

25

language is acquired in a context that sets it apart in people's minds from their ordinary experience of language.

This explicit knowledge ABOUT, however, does influence attitudes to language as strongly as folk-linguistic, but it is necessary to anticipate what is said about 'schemata' in Chapter 4 (p. 51) in order to show why this should be so. 'Schemata' concern the way in which human beings use the processes of the brain to interpret their experience. The brain can make a map, or better, a series of maps, of experience, using as its raw material anything in the life of an individual. Once made, the maps become the basis for his interpretation of the world, the objects he sees, the events that happen to him, and the people with whom he comes in contact. Very young children spend much of their energy in building up these maps, or 'schemata', about the solidness, or hardness and softness, or lightness or heaviness, of objects. The ability to use the relationship between objects for information about size and distance also depends upon such 'schemata'. It is as though the schemata provide a check list of the properties of objects that serve to identify them as books, chairs, tables and so on. In this way, they form a vital part of our ability to make sense of the physical world about us. Surrealist painting or psychedelic effects in films can create great unease in a viewer, because they deliberately set out to contradict what his schemata tell him about the behaviour of objects in space. In fact, the ability to make sense of experience, to interpret what is seen and heard and felt, depends ultimately upon the schemata that are set up for the purpose.

Acquiring knowledge of a language, therefore, is a process of setting up the relevant schemata for the production and decoding of discourse, and Professor Halliday's 'models of language' point to one kind of schemata that the speaker has to develop for the purpose. They are the schemata which enable him to work out the functional possibilities that his language makes available to him. Correspondingly, learning language in a particular culture leads to the building up of comparable schemata that form the basis of the speaker's folk-linguistic and thus enable him to interpret the acts of languaging in which he is involved. Learning a foreign language or being taught about 'English' requires the building of further schemata that then contribute in turn to his folk-linguistic by providing new possibilities for interpreting language.

In curriculum terms, learning a foreign language often divides into the business of acquiring the necessary syntax and vocabulary, 'oral performance', and getting to know 'the culture of the country'. A 'direct method' approach, with or without the language laboratory, aims at integrating acquisition and performance, but as a very experienced Head of Modern Languages put it, "What you join together in the lab., the Public Examiner puts asunder". From the point of view of this chapter, however, what matters is the individual's *recollected* experience of studying foreign languages at school. For the majority, it is still a recollection of learning syntax and vocabulary in order to translate 'sentences' and do 'unseens' and this remains something quite distinct from being able to use the knowledge so gained for speaking or writing in real situations. Many people leave school convinced that what is learnt from the printed page and then written down is the most important part of studying language, and this conviction underlies the widespread habit of identifying the study of language itself with the learning of syntax and vocabulary. The short-cut that is established between learning the patterns of a language, and any other aspect of language learning, has a powerful and lasting influence upon folk-linguistic ideas about the kind of 'knowledge' that 'knowledge ABOUT language' can be.

What 'English Language' contributes to folk-linguistic ideas of 'Knowledge about Language' is a more complex matter. In one sense, many people would be surprised to hear that it contributed anything, because, to them, 'Knowledge about a language' can only mean knowledge of the patterns of a language other than their own. From the point of view of this chapter, however, there are three main elements in 'English Language' work that do add to people's schemata for interpreting 'knowledge about language'. These three elements are the text-book analysis of points of grammar and usage, including what is commonly understood by 'parsing'; the philological concern with the history of words, their roots and derivations, and with the history of the language; and what can best be called the 'prescriptive approach', which includes the 'plain words' notion of usage, and an underlying emphasis upon the idea of 'Good English'.

Whatever the extent of their present use by teachers of English, they have undoubtedly been responsible for some of the most widely held

27

views in our culture about the nature and function of language. More relevant to this context is the effect that they have had upon ideas about the study of language. The first of them, however, raises a question that has so far been carefully avoided: what is meant by the word "grammar"? Like 'nature' and 'freedom', and 'education', 'grammar' is used to cover an enormous number of different things from details of orthography, like the placing of an apostrophe, to the whole range of explicit information about language that is given out under the heading of 'English Language'. At times, people do use it to refer to the structure of sentences; at others, they will mean by it something like the ability to handle written English according to predilections of the speaker. As one headmistress of a Junior School put it, "When they come to us, they have no grammar." These various uses of the word are not easy to disentangle, and readers who are interested in pursuing the matter further can find an entertaining attempt to do so by Professor Quirk in his book, *The Use of English*.

The rudimentary form of analysis of sentences that many people know as 'parsing' is the most widespread of all models of grammatical enquiry. In fact, it remains the only model that the majority of people possess for the explicit study of English. 'Grammar' is 'nouns, verbs, and adjectives', 'doing grammar' is learning to use such labels correctly. 'Doing grammar' is like a lot of other work at school, a matter of learning the facts and then using them to do formal exercises. 'Grammar' is remembered as a school subject, something quite unconnected with using language as a competent speaker/hearer, and is linked in people's minds with recollections of studying a foreign language. The final effect is to leave many people with the impression that 'grammar' has as much to do with real language as 'sentences using the pluperfect subjunctive' has with asking your way to the Cherbourg car-ferry. The following quotation comes from the report of a teacher who was taking part in the class-room trials of "Language in Use". He asked his class what they understood by the word, 'English', and their replies made it clear that they were not "aware that it is a *language*, that it is for expressing and transmitting ideas. They thought of it as a school subject divided into 'reading', 'poetry', and 'composition'." In another school they might well have added 'grammar'.

With the second of these three elements, the philological, the emphasis usually falls upon individual words, where they have come from, and how their original meaning is related to the meaning that they now carry. It has two distinct effects, however, on attitudes to knowledge about language. The focus upon words leads to the idea that language and 'words' are virtually synonymous. A popular account of the history of the language, like Simeon Potter's *Our Language*, is almost exclusively concerned with changes in the use and meaning of words, treated in isolation from each other, and the use of the word 'language' in the title is an interesting example of the degree to which common thinking about language does regard 'words' and 'language' as virtually synonymous. At the same time, this emphasis tends to be concentrated upon what is often called the 'original' or 'proper', or 'true' meaning of a word. Once again, the word in question will be treated in isolation from its occurrence in a grammatical context or particular way of speaking or writing. Together, these two aspects of the philological preoccupation with words supports the general idea that knowledge about the language is essential knowledge about the meaning of the words of the language, treated without context and in a historical perspective. It also leads many people to believe that the most important kind of knowledge about language is to be found between the covers of a dictionary.

The concentration upon 'original' meanings is accompanied by a very strong belief in the idea of an 'original' condition of the language that was, in some sense or other, preferable to, or superior to, its present condition. Change in the meaning of words is invariably seen as a corruption or debasement of their 'true' meaning and therefore a threat to the effectiveness with which the language is able to convey precision of meaning. This attitude to changes of meaning is but one expression of an underlying belief that all linguistic change is inherently undesirable, because it damages the ideal form of the language. The duty of educated users of the language is to maintain the pattern of usage which they judge to embody that ideal. The coining of new words is frowned upon, a watch is kept for usages that come into the language from other varieties of English, especially American English. There is a resistance to the use of technical language, and fear is expressed that the language is being diminished through the loss of some particular distinction like that between 'may' and 'might'. While there may/might be particular examples of each one of these cases that are in themselves undesirable, taken together they represent some of the most important ways in which

29

a language measures up to the ever-changing needs of the people who speak it. Moreover, those who hold to this general position do not put forward any criteria for assessing what is and is not desirable that would be acceptable from an objectively linguistic point of view.

At its most extreme, this attitude sees such linguistic change as a sign of the moral decadence of the nation. Evidence of this is readily available in the letter columns of *The Times*, or *The Daily Telegraph*, or *Radio Times*. From this point of view, knowledge about language is a matter of knowing what is 'the proper use of English' in order to single out those groups and persons who constitute a danger to the moral or intellectual well-being of the nation, through their mis-use of language. This may or may not be a desirable activity, but it is clear from their comments that the majority of those who undertake the task have no more than their unmodified folk-linguistic to guide them in their assessment of what is, or is not, damaging to a language. The result is that their efforts seldom amount to more than a witch-hunt after any usage that does not conform to their own social prejudices.

It is at this point that the philological element merges into the prescriptive. The most important single feature of the prescriptive element in 'English Language' work is the degree to which it turns one way of using written English into an arbitrary measure of all usage, written and spoken. It leaves a majority of people convinced that spoken language is but a fragmentary, or incomplete, or even incorrect, version of written language. People will say that "Spoken English has no grammar", or that "This class just can't talk in sentences", or that "Talk is all very well, but it doesn't have to be logical like writing". "The proper use of the English Language" or some master pattern of 'correct usage' is the feeling underlying such comment—that talk is best which can be seen to approximate most closely to the forms of the written language. The relationship between speech and writing is discussed in detail in Chapter 9, but the essential point is the degree to which work on English language at school can leave a permanent impression in people's minds that only written language has validity as language.

In addition, there is the matter of what Professor Halliday calls "... the 'ritual' model of language". He defines this as "... the image of language internalised by those for whom language is a means of showing how well one was brought up; it downgrades language to the level of table-manners".

He goes on to say that language conceived of, and used, according to this model, ". . . serves to define and delimit a social group". In the context of teaching and learning, this model manifests itself in two distinct but related ways, and in both cases, teachers of all kinds and all subjects are involved. There is the straightforward importation of this model into the learning situation, so that pupils and students are made to feel inadequate through their inability to conform to its requirements. The prescriptive element is expressed through the teacher's demand for a 'good English' that embodies features of the language which "define and delimit" the social group to which he belongs. Study of teachers' attitudes in Primary Schools has shown that the child's ability to use the linguistic table-manners his teacher expects is a key element in determining not only the teacher's attitude to the child, but his assessment of his potential as a learner. In the course of their work in developing *Language in Use*, the authors of this book have found such assessment at every level of the educational system.

A very large number of teachers use the written language of their students and pupils as a means of assessing how well they have been brought up educationally. For them, particular patterns of usage, like proper use of an impersonal passive; the ability to use qualifying elements like 'probably', or 'considerably'; the ability to shape factual statements tentatively; or the ability to express personal response to mundane experience, serve to 'define and delimit a social group', in this case those who are worthy of being educated. Much common-room demand for a 'clear, concise, and intelligible English' is an expression of the wish that students' experience of language should coincide with that of their teachers. This manifestation of the prescriptive element is built into the very notion of a 'good examination answer' and underlies much of the comment upon the use of language that occurs in the subject reports of the public examination boards. (See the quotation on p. 113). It is akin to the wide-spread popular belief in a 'plain English' that will serve all the needs of communicating information in writing. The linguistic table-manners that are thought to reveal the presence of this universally applicable 'plain English', "define and delimit" the social group who are thought best suited to the staffing of the key institutions in our society, the Law, the Civil Service, Education, company administration, and so on.

The effect of the prescriptive element upon our folk-linguistic is thus complex and wide-ranging, as it defines for most people the essential characteristics of language in use. It leads them to believe that explicit knowledge about a language is primarily a matter of standards of acceptability, believed to be linguistic, but often covertly and unconsciously social or intellectual. In the special case of teachers it leads them to use an arbitrarily selected collection of ill-assorted linguistic features as a measure of student's fitness for learning and potential success in their field. In this context, the proper study of language becomes a matter of "the judgement of manners and the correction of taste", its best-known monuments, Gower's *Plain Words* and Fowler's *The King's English*.

Much explicit knowledge about language is acquired in such a way that it remains fragmented in the minds of those who come by it. Being very closely associated with school it often retains an air of unreality about it as though it does not really relate to anything outside the world of school and the exercises through which it was learnt. At the same time, it does have a marked and lasting effect upon people's attitudes to language, to knowledge about language, and to the activity of studying language. In this sense, it becomes part of their view of linguistic reality. In fact, for those who pass through the whole process of formal education to degree or certificate level, it can be the most influential element of all in shaping their folk-linguistic thinking about language. If one is a teacher it is, therefore, essential to be able to work out what effect the prescriptive element has had upon one's present and professional attitudes to language and its use in teaching and learning.

4

It is now time to consider the explicitly linguistic exploration of language and how this differs from all the other kinds of knowledge about language that have so far been discussed in this chapter. It is at this point that Linguistics makes its appearance. As a name for a field of academic study, it is still not at all widely known, and there is little common understanding of what its concerns might be. Linguistics is the scientific study of language, an established academic discipline comparable in its range of concerns to more familiar disciplines like Mathematics, or History, or Biology. This means that there are many divisions within the broad heading of Linguistics, and they have their own goals and a developed method of enquiry for pursuing them. What these divisions are, and how they relate to each other, is beyond the scope of this book, but readers who want to find out can turn to the titles suggested in the bibliography for this chapter. For the present, something needs to be said about the goals of Linguistics, and something also about the implications of the phrase, 'the scientific study of language'. To say that a study is 'scientific' can be alternatively intimidating, or damning, according to a reader's preconceptions about the type of exploration that this would involve. As far as the exploration of language is concerned it need be neither, and the aim of this section is to show why.

Like Psychology and Sociology, Linguistics in its present form is primarily a product of the twentieth century, and, like them, it came into being through the desire of many investigators to make use of the objective methods of Natural Science in new fields—in their case, the study of languages. The essential step was to treat the patterns of a language as the physicists would treat the properties of materials or the biologist the structure of organisms. The patterns of a language were to be the 'facts' by means of which general statements about the nature and function of language could be built up through a process of observation and experiment. In particular, the raw material for observation and analysis would be the patterns of language as they were used by those who spoke them as mother tongues. The emphasis was upon the analysis of real language, spoken in a particular place at a particular time. In a discussion of the basis of the subject, Professor Firth, the major figure in establishing modern linguistic studies in this country, put it this way,

> "synchronic linguistics first assumes there is such a thing as a language, secondly that it exists apart from the individual people who use it, and having made those two big assumptions ... it makes a third assumption, that a language can be said to exist in a given state. Synchronic linguistics then applies itself to the study of the elements and structure of the language in the given state."

Firth is here making use of a fundamental distinction in the study of language between a focus that is 'diachronic', that is, concerned with the history of a language, and one that is 'synchronic' and takes as its focus the patterns of a language at the moment an enquiry is made. The foundation of the philological study of language in the nineteenth century was the study of changes in the form of languages over long periods of time, whereas the study of languages at one point in time has been the foundation of the linguistic study of language in this century. At the present moment, a linguist would study, let us say, the 'elements and structure' of the English that is spoken by educated speakers of English born in the south-east of England. In common language terms, 'elements' are parts of speech and 'structure' is the way they are combined to make clauses and sentences. Alternatively, he might study the contemporary English of Indians who speak Indian English as a mother tongue. Whatever his interest, it will be with 'the elements and structure' of a language spoken at a particular point in time, by particular individuals, in a particular social and cultural context, what Firth refers to as ". . . a given language . . . in a given state".

The linguist, however, is not only interested in ascertaining and listing what these 'elements and structures' are. Were this the case, there would be little difference between the work of a much older tradition of linguistic description going back to the Greeks, and what is now done within the field of Linguistics. One of the most widely known examples of those older tradition is the perennial Kennedy's Latin Grammar, where all the 'elements' are classified and listed according to a rational scheme. Bradley's 'Arnold's Latin Prose Composition' or 'Marchant and Watson' is supposed to take care of the 'structures'. Another well-known example is provided by the grammatical information set out in the books of the *Teach Yourself* series. In neither case, however, is there very much evidence of a framework which would explain why the patterns of a language are as they are, and not otherwise. In the same way, the 'Grammatical', 'Philological', and 'Prescriptive' elements, described in the previous part of this chapter, all offer facts about English, but they only add up to a heap of unrelated details about 'elements and structure'. Consider for a moment this quotation from one of the Reith Lectures given by Professor Edmund Leach in 1967,

"Suppose you wanted to answer the question 'What is a motor-car?' You could, if you like, simply list several thousand individual parts by name. This would be a description of a sort, but it wouldn't be much use. What most people would want to know is how the thing works as a whole, and to explain that you would need to show just what connects up with what."

This points to the contrast between the older tradition and the Linguistic study of language as it has been developed in this century. What Kennedy gives you is your 'several thousand individual parts': what Linguistics exists to do is 'show just what connects up with what'.

There is another question, however. The quotation from Professor Firth suggests how the linguist sets out to show 'what connects up with what', by providing a framework within which he can describe 'how the thing works as a whole', but it does not say anything about why this is worth doing in the first place. Arguably, it is worth doing, because, like Everest, language 'is there'. As a distinguished academic once said to the author, "Strictly speaking, all academic enquiry is useless. Finding out is justification enough.' Unfortunately, in a field like the exploration of language, such a heroic assertion is no longer a sufficient justification, because it is a field that must take into account problems and needs other than the study of language for its own sake. In the case of this book, it is the problems and needs of teachers and pupils in the context of using language for learning, and two further quotations from Professor Firth can provide a more relevant answer from this point of view. In a paper concerned with the nature of the goals proper to the linguistic study of a language, he said that:

"the object of linguistic analysis is to make statements of meaning so that we may see how we use language to live."

In another context, he elaborated this by saying that,

"Linguistics . . . is mainly interested in persons and personalities as active participants in the creation and maintenance of cultural values."

In other words, the focus of linguistic enquiry may have to be upon the 'elements and structures' of language, but the purpose of describing them is to show how they are used by the speakers of those languages in going about the business of day-to-day living. Every one of us is involved in 'the creation and maintenance of cultural values', because everyone speaks a language, and it is through language that these values are transmitted and expressed.

This last quotation, however, does raise the problem of what is meant by 'culture'. This word is as awkward and slippery as 'grammar' or 'values', but Firth means by it something like the network of values, attitudes and beliefs that gives a society or part of a society, a recognisable identity. In the words of a great nineteenth-century British anthropologist, Sir Edward Tylor, it includes:

> "Knowledge, belief, art, morals, law, custom, and any other capabilities and habits acquired by man as a member of society."

From the point of view of the linguistic study of language, the most important phrase in this quotation is 'capabilities and habits acquired by man as a member of society'. The uniqueness of language derives from the fact that it is, at one and the same time, a capability man acquires through growing up as a member of a particular society and the major means by which he can acquire all the other capabilities that Tylor mentions. As Firth implies, language is the primary agency through which we express our understanding of such things as knowledge and belief and art, and thus is truly indispensable 'in the creation and maintenance of cultural values'. Moreover, many of those values depend upon the very 'elements and structure' of the language itself, so that the process of acquiring one's own language is also a process of acquiring the 'cultural values' of the society to which one belongs. In fact, the position can be put as strongly as this:

> "Indeed, language itself is a complex inventory of all the ideas, interests and occupations that take up the attention of the community."

This was written by a most important figure in the development of linguistic studies, the American, Edward Sapir. Put this way, it is clear that the linguistic study of language so defined cannot proceed very far without facing the fact that it is the least independent of disciplines, because the activity of language is never an end in itself, but always a means to the creation and maintenance of the fabric of individual lives and of particular human communities.

36

The linguist's immediate goal is often the objective and detailed description of a language, its sound patterns, its elements and its structure. In the process, he may throw much light upon the nature and function of language, because he is trying to show how it is organised internally. The ultimate goal of linguistic enquiry, however, is to be able to 'show how we use language to live'. This is to say that enquiry into the nature and function of language must end up by contributing to a better understanding of the nature and function of human society. In the words of Malinowski:

"... language functions as a link in concerted human activity, as a piece of human behaviour."

It is a middle, with its beginning and end in the activities of individual human beings, activities that are primarily social, for they involve the individual in a continuous process of relationship with other human beings. From the point of view of an activity like teaching and learning, therefore, the relevant questions concern the relationship of 'beginning' and 'end' to 'middle'. The 'elements and structure' that make up the 'middle', the internal organisation of language, need only concern the teacher, therefore, insofar as they illuminate the ways in which he and his students use language as 'active participants' of learning situations.

The common idea of linguistics as a kind of glorified sentence analysis is thus a gross over-simplification of its concerns. It is this idea that makes it hard for the teacher to see how the linguistic study of language can be relevant to the problems of the class-room. An alternative way of looking at things is to see that there are different kinds of study possible within the broad domain of linguistic enquiry and that what distinguishes them is the purpose for which the enquiry is undertaken and the sort of explicit knowledge about language to which they lead. Moreover, it is helpful to see that the domain of linguistic enquiry is itself much wider than the conventional limits of the academic subject called General Linguistics. It is proper to think of Linguistic Studies as a domain that embraces all aspects of serious and explicit intellectual enquiry into language. It would cover the interest in language that is necessarily a part of any study of the individual or society, be it psychological, sociological or anthropological.

This has been recognised in the last two decades by the emergence of psycho-linguistics and socio-linguistics, the former very much concerned with language acquisition, the latter interested in such things as the relationship between home background and command of a language, or the way in which judgements of social class are relatable to speech patterns. The reasoning behind these developments is that there are problems like language acquisition or the effects of social background upon language which require the participation of two social sciences for their solution. Psychology can describe the processes by which language is acquired, but only Linguistics can describe what is acquired. Similarly, Sociology can describe the background, but not the patterns of language use that are relatable to it. Unfortunately, life is a lot messier than this tidy division of academic responsibility would have it. The setting up of such hybrid disciplines does not help to further understanding of language if it encourages people to focus solely upon its individual, or its social, or its linguistic, aspect to the exclusion of the other two. What the teacher needs is to see that the broad field of Linguistic Studies embraces all three aspects and that all three are relevant to the linguistic problems of teaching and learning.

Within the general field of Linguistic Studies, there is a 'subject linguistics' that gives its name to university departments. Normally called General Linguistics departments, they are primarily concerned with the training of students to undertake the linguistic study of language. They make their selection from the range of possible Linguistic Studies with this end in mind. The centre of their activities is properly the systematic and explicit analysis of the patterns of natural languages, grammatical and phonological. Only a small part of their concerns, therefore, are likely to seem at all relevant to the problems of teaching and learning. What the teacher needs is a selection from the whole range of Linguistic Studies expressly made with these problems in mind and this selection can be called Language Study to differentiate it from all other kinds of exploration into the nature and function of language. The linguistic problems particular to teaching and learning are obviously very different from the problems that exercise the professional linguist. It is hardly surprising, therefore, that a course in Language Study would look very different from a degree or diploma course syllabus in General Linguistics. In particular, the focus must be upon the interaction between the individual, the social, and the linguistic aspects of lan-

38

guage rather than any one of the three for itself alone. An inescapable consequence of the present state of Linguistic Studies is that many of the topics most relevant to Language Study are the least well understood. For instance, a great deal can be done to show how the grammatical patterns of 3- or 6- or 9-year-old differ from those of adult speakers of the language, but what must concern the teacher is why they differ, and here the results of linguistic enquiry are likely to be tentative and suggestive rather than cut-and-dried.

If Language Study is that selection from the whole field of Linguistic Studies appropriate to the exploration of language in the context of teaching and learning, then the volume called *Language in Use* produced by the authors of this book for Schools Council represents one way of making Language Study available to those who have not previously considered language from a linguistic point of view, be they teachers, teachers-in-training, students or pupils. Perhaps the best way of showing the relationship between these four categories of exploring language is to take the analysis of sentences and see how it appears in the context of each of them. Properly conducted, the analysis of sentences should show how various possible combinations of 'elements and structure' express what Professor Halliday calls 'the meaning potential' in a language. As we commonly use the phrase, however, we do not distinguish between the knowledge about language that this analysis provides, and the ability to perform the analysis. The product of the analysis is relevant to the whole range of Linguistic Studies, but the ability to use the specialised techniques of linguistic description in order to produce the analysis is particularly the concern of academic 'subject linguistics'. While the knowledge that derives from the analysis will be relevant to most aspects of Language Study, the ability to perform the analysis will be needed by comparatively few teachers. Finally, analysing sentences is in no sense a necessary part of exploring language in the class-room, as *Language in Use* demonstrates.

Language Study, then, takes the needs of teachers and pupils as its criterion of relevance for selecting particular topics for exploration out of the whole range of Linguistic Studies. It recognises that teachers are interested in two kinds of knowledge about language, what will help them to understand the part played by language in the processes of learning and teaching and what will best show them how this part can be related to language as a feature of living, individual and social. A teacher will want to know about the way in which human beings acquire language; how they extend their command over it; what part is played by background in determining pupils' capacity to use language; the degree to which the educational system develops its own expectations about effective use of language; the way in which a subject-centred curriculum makes demands upon the linguistic competence of learners; the linguistic limitations of the 'essay' form as a means of assessing what has been learnt. Topics such as these would all be part of understanding how successful learning is dependent upon a pupil's ability to use the language for learning that it expected of him.

The other side of the matter, however, is to see such topics as particular examples of characteristics that belong to all language. By setting them in the context of the human use of language, the teacher can see why these topics are so important to his understanding of language in the class-room. In this sense, he will be concerned with all three faces of language. He needs to see how the individual uses the elements and structure of a natural language to categorise, order, and interpret his experience of the world, and in order to do this he will have to look at the means by which that language is acquired. At the same time, he needs to see how individuals draw upon those elements and structure to create relationships with each other, to give identity to groups and institutions within their society, and thus to maintain its fabric. Finally, he needs to take a look at the internal organisation of language itself in order to see that language is 'meaning potential', an enormously elaborate system for constructing and conveying meanings. The rest of this book is primarily concerned with the individual and social faces of language, because these two faces are most easily relatable to the everyday problems of teaching and learning. They can demonstrate the relevance of exploring language for any teacher and develop the desire to go on and tackle the third face of language, its internal organisation. This is a topic so large and so unfamiliar that it will require a book to itself.

FURTHER READING

Y. R. Chao, *Language and Symbolic Systems* (C.U.P.), Chapters 1–5.

P. S. Doughty, *Current Attitudes to Written English*, in Nuffield Papers in Linguistics and English Teaching (Longman).

J. R. Firth, *The Tongues of Men* (O.U.P.).

M. A. K. Halliday, "General Linguistics and its application to language teaching", in *Patterns of Language*, Angus McIntosh and M. A. K. Halliday (Longman).

M. A. K. Halliday, *An Outlook on Modern English* (O.U.P.).

J. Lyons, "The Structure of Language", Chapter 2 of *An Introduction to Theoretical Linguistics* (C.U.P.).

E. Sapir, *Language* (Rupert Hart-Davis).

Three   The language we acquire

"The ability to learn language is so deeply rooted in man that children learn it even in the face of dramatic handicaps."—E. H. Lenneberg.

"They could hardly speak English."—Retired Headmistress, about former pupils in Oxfordshire.

1

The human brain is a language-learning brain, so that human beings, in the first few years of life, have the power to create for themselves, out of the language they hear, language they can use. Ordinarily, that is unless the brain is gravely damaged, the process of growing up in an environment where language is in everyday use is a sufficient condition for this learning to take place, so that most children acquire the basis of language by the age of five.

The folk-linguistic notion of this process would seem to suggest that acquiring language is an experience rather like catching measles, with the difference that some people catch a 'good' version of a language, while others, less fortunate, catch a 'bad' version. As Peter Doughty pointed out in his discussion of folk-linguistic in Chapter 1, 'good' and 'bad' are, in this popular view, usually equated with accents that are socially approved or disapproved of, although it was once claimed in an article in *The Guardian* that, at all levels, the British learn "to speak their language less well than many other nations, including most conspicuously the French."

Accounts of the process of language-learning given by linguists tend to concentrate on describing the grammatical stages that a child's language goes through as he progresses from his first word, at about nine months, to his first two-word utterances at about eighteen months, and beyond that to mastery of the basic sentence forms. "Three Processes in the Child's Acquisition of Syntax", by Bellugi and Brown, offers a good example of this kind of observation and description.

For the teacher, however, in his concern with the child as learner,

42

there are two important aspects of the process of acquiring language. What are the factors at work to make the language acquired by any one individual the highly personal possession that it is? What is the relationship between the language acquired in the first few years of life and the ability subsequently to use language for learning?

2

A baby will normally be born into a small group that is part of a larger speech community, consisting of a number of people who have an established pattern of relationships with each other, and who are already using language to live by. The size and membership of this group, usually a family group, will vary according to its whereabouts in the world. Whereas, in one locality, an only child may find himself living with his mother and father in an insulated family unit, elsewhere a family may consist of several brothers and sisters, with perhaps grandparents and other relatives living with them. Contact with other members of the family, such as brothers and sisters of the parents, and their children, may be anything from close and frequent to distant and occasional. The number of other human beings with whom an infant is brought into contact at birth, and with whom, as with a peer-group, he establishes contact in the first few years of life, will thus vary, as will the pattern of relationships they have with him and with each other. The amount, and the kind, of language produced by the daily working-out of those relationships will have far-reaching consequences for language-learning, for it is during these first years of life that the foundations of language are laid. Never again will the child be in such intimate and dependent relationship with those from whom he is learning. Never again will he be able to devote so much time uninterruptedly to the process.

The language of his immediate family group will be the language of a larger speech community—English, or French, or Gujerati, or any of the 3000 or so languages to be found in the world. More precisely, the language of the family, according to where it is located geographically or socially within a community, will be a variety of this language.

There may, of course, be more than one language spoken within the family. Some countries, politically speaking, contain more than one

43

speech community, whether or not there is more than one 'official' language, so that children may be brought up speaking more than one language. Or the marriage may be 'linguistically' mixed, with the children brought up bi-lingually, that is, apparently given the opportunity to master two language systems at the same time. It is necessary to say 'apparently' because there is some evidence to suggest that two languages acquired under circumstances such as this do not, in fact, exist side-by-side, co-equally in the brain, with the individual being able to draw with equal readiness upon both, or either. The conditions governing the acquisition of the languages appear to exert an influence upon later facility to use them. For example, the need to use language in a context which has associations with the child's relationship with its mother will mean that the language of the mother will be more readily available. This indicates the subtlety of the process by which language is acquired.

This process is essentially an inter-active process, the innate capacity of the brain for language-learning interacting with the language of the environment. It is, perhaps, necessary to emphasise that it is the same whether the child is growing up on the banks of the Thames, the banks of the Mersey, or the banks of the Amazon. Basically, this process may be seen as one in which the child learns to pick out and discriminate between more and more of the elements of language, the sounds, the rhythms, the intonations of which it is composed. In English, there is a difference between 'pin' and 'bin'; between 'I scream' and 'ice-cream'; between 'Coming?' asked as a question and 'Coming' uttered as a statement. They represent some of the distinctions, some of the kinds of distinction, that the child learns, and learns to make.

Although there is evidence to suggest that the child learns intonation patterns before it learns words, it is in the building of sounds into words, and words into utterances, that progress in language learning is traditionally recognised. " Is yours talking yet?' is the question inevitably asked by the parents of a child who has just uttered a recognisably linguistic sound, although the ability to reproduce the meaningful sounds of a language is not necessarily an indicator of how much language has been learnt. There is a time-lag between being able to recognise, and attach meaning to, words and sequences of words, and being able to use them. Thus, a child who knows that a question is being asked, in the sense that he knows that a par-
44

ticular kind of response is required, or knows that he himself wants to ask a question, may not be able to put together a sequence involving the kind of word order needed for "Can I have . . . ?" or "Do you want . . . ?"

However, the child learns to put words together, two at a time, three at a time, until he can eventually put together utterances that follow the grammatical patterns of the language spoken in the home. Such patterns, whose regularities are known to the linguist as 'rules', occur in every variety of every language, whether or not they have been observed and codified by a linguist or not. Despite those who say of some children's language "They haven't any grammar", or "Their grammar is so poor", the fact is that any and all language must have a grammar in order to function. But the child does not have to wait until he can construct gramatically complete utterances before he can make himself understood by means of language. "I want . . .", pointing to the object, is as meaningful as "I want a sweet". Language is not the only means of communication that people have at their disposal. Bodily gestures, such as pointing, waving, or shaking the fist, and facial expressions, like smiling or scowling, carry meaning for people as they react and relate to others. Language is learnt in a kind of syntactic relationship with such non-linguistic features of the environment, as they are used by the people in the environment going about the business of living.

3

The relationships which exist between the people in the child's environment, and the reasons for which they use language in the working-out of those relationships, constitute the matrix within which the language of the environment functions. Peter Doughty has more to say about the part played by language in social relationships in Chapter 5. The child learns, by being exposed to it, how language is used, what language is used for, and he comes to learn how to use it himself for similar purposes. "Come in now, it's tea-time" shows him that language can be used not only to convey information but also to control his behaviour; "Go away, mummy's got a headache" not only to control behaviour but to express feelings.

In *Relevant Models of Language*, Professor Halliday emphasises that, "The child knows what language is because he knows what language does", so that, through his own experience of language, the child becomes "subconsciously aware that language has many functions that affect him personally." Among these functions, Professor Halliday suggests, are:

(a) Language for getting things done, for satisfying one's needs—which the child learns perhaps as the "I want..." kind of language.
(b) Language for controlling the behaviour of others—the "don't do that" kind of language.
(c) Language for getting on with other people—the "kiss mummy goodnight" or "will you play with me?" kind of language.
(d) Language for expressing personality, or individuality—the "I'm going to be an engine-driver when I grow up" kind of language.
(e) Language for finding things out, for exploring the environment—the "why?", the "what for?", the "tell me..." of the inquisitive child.
(f) Language for imaginative purposes—"let's pretend..." or "once upon a time...."
(g) Language for conveying information—the "I've got something to tell you" kind of language, whether that something is about persons, states, objects, or abstractions, in the world.

To have the chance of using language for all these purposes, the child must, first of all, be able to see for himself that language can be used for them, and then be given the opportunity to acquire the necessary linguistic means by hearing the appropriate forms used around him. If the relationsips of those about him are conducted in such a way as to eliminate language, especially in the means by which adults seek to control his behaviour, then he will be denied such opportunities. He will come to learn not so much what language can be used for, as what it cannot.

Language, as it mediates in every aspect of life, will be used for many functions at a time, and the child will learn to respond to them without conscious awareness of this functional diversity. "Come here...give me that...what have you been up to... didn't I tell you not to do that...you'll make mummy cross...I want you to get ready for bed now...it's bed-time..."

And from time to time may come a comment that implies something about the speaker's view of the appropriacy of language. "Don't

46

interrupt" not only defines the relationship between two people, it also reflects the way that one of them thinks that language should enter into the relationship. "Do you have to ask so many questions? Mummy's got a headache", not only reveals something about a person's feelings. It also says that there are inappropriate times for using language to find things out. "If I hear your voice again . . ." uttered as a threat in a railway carriage, is not only seeking to control behaviour. It also carries with it a notion of the impropriety of expressing personality through language in a public place. "Don't be silly", or "Stop day-dreaming", as comments upon public or private flights of fancy, place restrictions on the use of language for imaginative purposes.

At another level, "because I say so" is significantly different from "because it's wrong" or "because you oughtn't". The former remains firmly within the personal relationship of, say, mother and child, while the other two at least hint at the possibility of relating behaviour to standards derived from outside. And, at the same time, the use of the modal word "ought" or the abstraction "wrong" give the child the opportunity of acquiring a language in which behaviour can be discussed at levels of abstraction above the immediate situation. In the same way, any answers to "why" which take the form, say "Because if you don't you might . . . and then . . ." demonstrate to the child that language is there for asking questions and getting answers, and give him the means of considering, and discussing, cause and effect for himself.

Various features of family life, such as the reciting of nursery rhymes or the reading of stories to young members, reading aloud from newspapers at breakfast and discussing topical items of news, discussing holiday or other plans, watching and afterwards discussing television programmes, may combine with the other purposes for which language is used to create the language environment in which an individual child will spend his language-formative years. These years are short, and the language learning that takes place is very concentrated. Factors at work in the environment which bear upon the kind of language acquired by each individual, under these circumstances, are both subtle and complex.

One such factor is the degree to which a child is exposed to 'undiluted' adult company and language; in other words, the opportunity he has, early in life, of learning what adults talk about, and how. In

47

this respect, only children, or eldest children until the arrival of a younger brother or sister, appear to have an advantage which may help to explain a statistic quoted in *Dear Lord James* (ed. Tyrrell Burgess, Penguin, p. 23) about the student population of a College of Education. "Half the students were, in fact, only or first-born children and a further 35 per cent were the second born in their families." Likewise, there is evidence that twins, who are apt to spend much of their time in each other's company, experience delay in acquiring forms of the language used by adults in the family.

Another factor which bears on the language-learning process, in all its subtlety, is that no two people, even identical twins, occupy the same place in a family environment. They will inevitably have a different set of relationships with other members of the family, so that they will be the focus of different linguistic interactions, at the receiving end of different forms of language.

Older children will be told, "Don't do that, you're older than he is", or "Don't tease/hurt/bully him—you're bigger than he is," or "You shouldn't do that . . . you should look after him." Boys will be differentiated from girls. "Little boys don't cry/play with dolls/hit little girls," or "Little girls don't fight/play with guns/climb trees."

The mother-daughter relationship may perhaps encourage possibilities of language use which tend in our culture to be eliminated in the father-son. "You'll have to grin and bear it," contrasts with "Come and tell Mummy all about it." "Come and help mummy set the table" may well be a collaborative effort, requiring plenty of inter-actional talk. "Help daddy wash the car", or some other male job, may, on the other hand, involve comparatively little interaction.

An eldest son will thereby have opportunity for learning a language significantly different from that which his young sister can learn, precisely because the language with which he is interacting will be different. It is considerations like this which ensure that the language acquired by any human being is a unique inheritance. It is an inheritance because he is endowed, as a human being, with the capacity to learn language merely by growing up in an environment in which language is being used round him. It is unique, because, as we have seen, no two people occupy identical places in an environment where language learning is taking place, and this must mean that the language learnt is unique to the individual.

It follows that the individual's language is something in which he has a great deal, virtually his whole life, invested. This was well illustrated by Bernard Coard in his booklet, "How the West Indian child is made educationally sub-normal in the British school system". Commenting on the fact that the West Indian child is liable to be told that his language is second-rate, Mr. Coard continues, "Namely, the only way he knows how to speak, the way he has always communicated with his parents and family and friends; the language in which he has expressed all his emotions, from joy to sorrow; the language of his innermost thoughts and ideas, is 'the wrong way to speak.' A man's language is part of him. It is his only vehicle for expressing his thoughts and feelings. To say that his language and that of his entire family and culture is second-rate, is to accuse him of being second-rate."

4

This is a very different matter from acknowledging that children born to grow up in some family environments are at a disadvantage when it comes to meeting the demands of school, compared with children from other kinds of environment. The emphasis here is not upon the comparative worth of human beings, and their language, but upon the relationship between language for living and language for learning. Professor Bernstein has done more than anyone else to explore the linguistic basis of educational failure, and to examine its relationship to social class. In the article, "A Critique of the Concept of Compensatory Education", which he contributed to *Education for Democracy*, he illustrates one aspect of the way in which this works:

> "Mothers in the middle-class, and it is important to add not all, relative to the working class (and again it is important to add not all by any means), place greater emphasis upon the use of language in socialising the child into the moral order, in disciplining the child, in the communication and recognition of feeling."

The key words are *place greater emphasis upon the use of language*. The "why's?" and "why not's?" of the growing child are more inclined to receive an answer like "Because if you do/don't . . . then you will/won't . . .", rather than, "because I say so", or simply "because".
"That's worse." "Why?" "It is."
"You mustn't do that." "Why not?" "You mustn't, that's all."

Bernstein would argue that it is in exchanges such as these that disadvantage in school begins because the language remains tied to the particular context in which it is used, it remains bound to the relationship which sponsored the exchange. Where reasons are advanced which break free from the context of the exchange, and appeal to some universal principle, such as, "If you do that you'll fall off and hurt yourself," or, "Because its' wrong to push", then the child "is oriented towards universalistic meanings which transcend a given context." And, as Bernstein points out, schools are institutions "concerned with the transmission and development of universalistic orders of meaning." Children whose early language experience does not take them far beyond the particularistic "because I say so" are not therefore so well endowed to meet the demands that school will make upon their language.

FURTHER READING

B. Bernstein, "A Critique of the Concept of Compensatory Education" in *Education for Democracy*, ed. D. Rubenstein and C. R. Stoneman (Penguin). [Reprinted in Bernstein, *Class, Codes and Control* (Routledge).]

R. Brown and U. Bellugi, "Three Processes in the Child's Acquisition of Syntax", in *New Directions in the Study of Language*, ed. E. H. Lenneberg (M.I.T.).

M. A. K. Halliday, "Language and Experience", in *The Place of Language* (Educational Review, Vol. 20, No. 2, February 1968).

M. A. K. Halliday, *Explorations in the Functions of Language* (Edward Arnold). See especially, "Relevant Models of Language" and "Language in a Social Perspective".

D. Lawton, *Social Class, Language and Education*, Chapter 2 (Routledge).

E. H. Lenneberg, "A Biological Perspective of Language", in *Language*, ed. R. C. Oldfield and J. C. Marshall (Penguin).

G. M. Thornton, *The Individual and his Development of a Language*, Papers in Linguistics and English Teaching, Series II (Longman).

A. Wilkinson, *The Foundations of Language*, Chapters VI and VII (O.U.P.).

Four   Language and experience

1

Learning to live and learning to language are virtually synonymous. We begin, almost as soon as we are born, to register and store, arrange and organise, impressions of what we encounter in our environment. Language enters into this process as soon as the growing child becomes aware of it, so that we begin, early in life, to build up a map, or rather a catalogue, of our experiences. When, in the course of our daily lives, we encounter something that is familiar, we draw upon our recollections of past experiences, our stored expressions, in order to handle the new experience.

Mary Douglas, in *Purity and Danger*, describes the process like this:

"... it seems that whatever we perceive is organised into patterns for which we, the perceivers, are largely responsible. Perceiving is not a matter of passively allowing an organ—say of sight or hearing—to receive a ready-made impression from without, like a palette receiving a spot of paint. Recognising and remembering are not matters of stirring up old images of past impressions. It is generally agreed that all our impressions are schematically determined from the start. As perceivers we select from all the stimuli falling on our sense only those which interest us, and our interests are governed by a pattern-making tendency, sometimes called schema. In a chaos of shifting impressions, each of us constructs a stable world in which objects have recognisable shapes, are located in depth, and have permanence. In perceiving we are building, taking some cues, and rejecting others. The most acceptable cues are those which fit most easily into the pattern that is being built up. Ambiguous ones tend to be treated as if they harmonised with the rest of the pattern. Discordant ones tend to be rejected. If they are accepted the structure of assumptions has to be modified. As learning proceeds objects are named. Their names then affect the way they are perceived next time: once labelled they are more speedily slotted into pigeon-holes in future."

In her book, *The Anatomy of Judgement*, M. L. Johnson Abercrombie gives a detailed account of the way in which we operate with schemata, and discusses how we organise experiences of sight, sound, touch, taste and smell; how we thereby divide up and impose

51

order on our environment; and how we categorise people and their behaviour as a basis for personal relationships.

To take one of her examples, let us suppose that we are choosing an apple from a dish. The basis of the choice is "our schemata of apples . . . compounded of impressions received by many sense organs, of colour, shape, size and texture as seen with the eyes; shape, size and texture, coolness and weight as felt by the hands; texture and coolness by the teeth and tongue; smell and taste; the rattle of the pips when shaken, or the crunch when bitten detected by the ear." And so we choose what we predict is going to be, for us, the best apple.

Suppose, however, that they are not our apples, but that we have been offered one by somebody else, so that we do not feel free to choose what we suspect is the best apple? Other schemata come into play. They will help us decide whether to take the nearest, or the smallest, because it is 'polite'; or whether we ought to take one at all, especially if we are very young, with mother at hand who perhaps thinks that "green apples are bad for you". Thus we try to predict what is expected of us by reference to recollections of similar past experiences which have been arranged and schematised almost like a filing-system.

There is an old story about a railway booking-clerk who was asked, by a small boy buying a ticket, whether his pet tortoise would have to be paid for. The clerk consulted his schedule, and eventually delivered himself of the judgement: "Dogs is dogs and cats is dogs, but that there tortoise is an insect and you don't pay for it."

The schedule he had consulted listed the categories of passengers, of animals, and of goods established by the railway company, together with the charges to be levied on each. In a similar way, we consult our own schedules of categories when confronted by something outside our experience. In fact, as Mary Douglas goes on to say, "As time goes on and experiences pile up, we make a greater and greater investment in our system of labels. So a conservative bias is built in. It gives us confidence. At any time we may have to modify our structure of assumptions to accommodate new experience, but the more consistent experience is with the past, the more confidence we can have in our assumptions. Uncomfortable facts which refuse to be fitted in, we find ourselves ignoring or distorting so that they do not disturb these established assumptions. By and large anything we take note of is preselected and organised in the very act of perceiving."

2

Early categorisation is accomplished through the agency of adults and any older children in the environment. In fact, the adults will be among the first of the features of the environment to be classified, with the mother first of all. The utterance of something like 'mama' is likely to be the linguistic evidence, to be followed later by 'dada' as another category. The use of this word may, in fact, indicate several stages of categorisation. Sometimes, it seems, all living things other than 'mama' may be categorised 'dada'. Thus, a small boy pointed to pigs on a farm and said 'dada'. When a toddler, at a later stage of development, referred to the man in an upstairs flat as 'daddy-up', one inference is that he had separated men into two categories of 'daddy'—upstairs and downstairs.

Following 'mama' and 'dada' will come other people in the immediate environment, first identified by name and then categorised into relationships such as brother and sister. After this will come categories of close relatives—grandparents, aunts and uncles, cousins. Sub-categories of maternal and paternal grandparents may sometimes be set up, with the use of different names to distinguish them, while the words 'aunt' and 'uncle' may signify a number of different categories of relationship that have to be learnt in respect of various friends and relatives. The word 'uncle', in particular, is used as a label for a wide variety of relationships. On the other hand, there may be no agreed, handy label for face-to-face communication where there is an imprecisely defined relationship. The commonest example in English is the difficulty that many people have in finding suitable modes of address for their parents-in-law.

But organising and classifying our experience in this way is not simply a process of assigning people or things to categories under one heading, such as 'mother', 'father', 'brother' or 'sister'. Members of the family will be put into more than one category by various criteria, such as men/women; boys/girls; grown-ups/children. With such categories will be associated the kinds of behaviour expected from and considered appropriate to them; the roles allocated to each within the home, and the kinds of task assigned to each; and the kinds of relationship permitted between them.

"You mustn't do that."
"Why not?"
"Because you're not old enough/a little boy/her brother . . ."

Other attributes of people which in time are classified include such things as habitual good or bad temper; state of health; physical characteristics such as height and weight; and tendencies such as clumsiness or tidiness. A brother, as well as being in the category 'brother'—in the family, not the religious sense—might also be classified by schemata that record him as fat, healthy, normally good-tempered, fair-haired, and given to clumsiness. But if someone were to say, "John's not very well today", other schemata, based on previous experience of states of 'unwellness', would operate to provide a prediction of what state John was in.

While learning to categorise the people living in his immediate environment, a child learns, by living with them and perceiving how they live, how those people use the space surrounding them. That is, how they divide it up, how they categorise it. (It is perhaps worth pointing out that the examples used to illustrate the argument in the following paragraphs derive from my own culture, since the categories we set up inevitably relate to the culture in which we grow up. Readers may care to substitute examples from their own cultures.)

This process means not merely learning that there may be rooms labelled 'kitchen', or 'bath-room', or 'dining-room', or 'lounge', but also of learning what is considered appropriate behaviour in each, and—perhaps even more important—who in the family has what rights in them, who regards them as 'territory'. Kitchens are usually places where mothers do such things as washing and cooking. But washing what—dishes, clothes, people, animals, bicycles? What meals, if any, are eaten in the kitchen? When, and for what, is the dining-room used? Is any room reserved, as the 'parlour' used to be, for certain events? (A character in Somerset Maugham's play *Sheppey* asks another character what she is doing. "Praying to God," is the answer. She replies. "Not in the sitting-room, Florrie.

I'm sure that's not right.") Not all bedrooms have the same status. Thus, a child may learn that while he is forbidden to enter his parents' bedroom his mother has unlimited rights of entry to his, and that he is expected to keep it 'tidy'—a category it often pays to learn early in life.

People in the environment divide not only space but time. At first, an infant divides his own time into sleeping and feeding, but he will gradually learn the pattern imposed upon time within his own family. There is the pattern of meal-times—breakfast time, lunch/ dinner time, tea/high tea/supper/dinner time—each with its own time, kind of meal, and associated expectations of behaviour. These include rules of attendance and punctuality, with permitted varia- tions at such times as weekends and holidays. He will learn how certain parts of the day are considered appropriate to particular activities. The earliest form of learning comes through phrases like, "Not now, it's bed-time", "Come on in, it's tea-time", or "No, mummy's resting." Afterwards, learning progresses from what time people like milkmen, postmen and doctors call, to what times are considered appropriate for other people, friends and relations, to drop in or ring up, so that if an aunt rings up to propose dropping in at nine o'clock on a Sunday evening, the reactions of other members of the family to her notion of appropriacy should be predictable.

We have seen how the child learns to categorise people in the environment by reference to different criteria—relationship, appear- ance, temperament, and so on, with words like brother, fat, healthy and fair doing the labelling. In the same way, he will learn to cate- gorise things in the environment according to different criteria; for example, who they belong to, what they are used for, or when they are used. At first, all things are to be played with. But gradually, through such injunctions as "You mustn't play with that", "Put that down, it's dangerous/you'll break it/it's not yours", "Give me that, it's mine", he learns that there is a category 'toy', but that there are also various categories of things not to be played with. He becomes acquainted with a range of objects that have functions in the life of the household—knives, forks, cups, plates, towels, sheets, and so on. He learns to categorise them as 'cutlery' or 'crockery', and then to sub-classify them in other ways, perhaps as 'best china' or 'kitchen spoon'. He will learn how some items are family posses- sions, for common use, but that some, like 'Johnny's mug' or 'father's

55

cup' are personal. Through questions like ,"Who's been using my tooth-brush?", he learns to set up categories of ownership—mine/yours/ours . . .

Clothing illustrates particularly well the complex system of cross-classification that has to be learnt, for it is classified under several headings: where on the body it is worn—underwear, footwear, and so on; what is made of—nylon/cotton/wool, giving nylons or woollies; when it is worn—outdoor/indoor, on holiday/for sport, in bed/in the garden, for best/everyday; how it is washed or cleaned—by hand/in lukewarm water, drip-dry, non-iron, dry-clean. So the child comes to regard as odd the neighbour who changes into pyjamas and dressing-gown, complete with a row of pens in the breast-pocket, as soon as he arrives home from work in the evening, as he had previously learnt that it was not normal to go and play in a muddy garden in his own new, albeit drip-dry, non-iron nylon pyjamas.

Items of clothing are usually personal, and the complex lending and borrowing rights that attach to some of them have to be learnt. What would be expected after "Can I borrow..." or "Lend me your..."? Is there anything that you would never lend, or borrow, under any circumstances?

Another important aspect of the way in which categories are set up as part of learning how to use language to live in a particular environment is that of learning how certain categories of things have to be kept in allocated places—toys in cupboards, clothes in drawers, food in the kitchen, worms in the garden, and so on. The learning will come through formulations like, "Put that away", where 'that' may be anything from a jig-saw to a sauce-bottle, and 'away' is the recognised place for keeping it. Injunctions like, "Take that out of here", or questions like, "Who left the tooth-paste in the dining-room?", are illustrations of the way in which organisation and categorisation are taught. They also begin to reveal what values are attached by adults in the family to particular aspects of behaviour. In a recent article in *The Observer*, a husband was reported as complaining about his wife, "She hides bills. Yesterday I found the electricity bill deep-frozen under the Irish stew in the fridge."

The child will learn very early, by understanding and associating
56

the expressions and gestures that accompany what he does, that some behaviour is acceptable and some is not. With certain kinds of behaviour he will learn to associate words like 'yes', 'good', 'right' or 'pleased'; while with other kinds of behaviour will be associated words like 'no', 'bad', 'wrong' or 'cross'. "Stop that", "You mustn't do that again", "That's a good boy", "Have you been naughty again?" and many other formulations will teach the child to set up categories of behaviour acceptable or unacceptable to authority.

Sooner or later, we come into contact with people outside the family group, and we learn that, if the family is 'we', other people are 'them'. We learn, too, in the same way that we learn how values are attached to certain forms of behaviour, how 'we' regard 'them'. Children in different parts of different societies will have ideas about 'them' mediated in different ways. 'Them-ness' may be, at one level, a matter of tribe, of race, of colour, of religion, of class. It may be impressed upon a child, for instance, that he is white, while 'they' are black, or vice-versa; that he is Catholic, with 'they' Protestant; that he is Jewish, with 'they' given various labels to denote non-Jewishness; or that he is a member of a privileged or non-privileged class, as the case may be. According to where he grows up, in which part of which community, he will inherit from his culture a complex of various levels, with various dimensions of 'otherness', and with various degrees of approval. Such categories may be at 'national' level, as in English or Australian; class, as in middle-class or working-class; race, as in white, black, or yellow; religious, as Methodist, Anglican or Muslim; regional, as in geordie, cockney or scouse; generational, as in teenagers, students; political, as in agitators and militants, tory or socialist. And many others. It might be theoretically possible to bring into relationship a number of differently organised schemata, and describe the teenage son of a marriage between a Jamaican and an Irish nurse in Liverpool as a "black, teenage, Irish, Catholic, working-class, socialist scouse."

The learning of such categories may come in the first instance through utterances like, "I don't like you playing with him", or "You're not to play with him." Reasons may be given in a form like, "They're not our sort/type/kind/class . . ." or "We don't mix with them/people like that/the likes of them . . ." This may be qualified by "They're common/vulgar/low" or "posh/snobbish/stuck up" or whatever attribute constitutes the vital defining category. In a

57

Nottingham village, where a new pit has been sunk and miners have come from Tyneside to work it, local mothers will not allow their children to play with the children of the miners "because they don't speak English". Other people are, by such devices, divided into those with whom it is permitted to make friends, visit and—later—marry, and those with whom such things are forbidden. The process is even more subtle than this account would seem to suggest, as is sometimes revealed by the reactions of parents to the announcement that their son or daughter intends to marry. These reactions will reveal the existence of underlying marriageable/not marriagable categories, as applied to someone who the son or daughter had innocently supposed to be acceptable.

This example illustrates the way in which a kind of *covert* categorisation underlies and influences much of our behaviour. For example, we derive from our particular culture a notion of what it is proper to eat, and what it is not. That is, we set up, implicitly, categories edible/non-edible under which we classify creatures like pigs, horses, frogs, eels, snakes, snails, grasshoppers and squids—all of which are 'edible' in one culture or another. What is proper to eat becomes what is usual to eat, and in this way we learn to set up a category labelled 'normal', as applied to food, so that while fish-fingers for breakfast is one man's normality, for another it is a culture shock.

But this does not apply merely to food. We set up a category 'normal' to cover virtually every aspect of human behaviour in our own society. "It's not normal" constitutes a powerful datum-line from and against which to evaluate future experiences. Language assists this process, as linguists have recently pointed out, by offering a choice between linked pairs of words, the usual or expected being the 'unmarked' case, with the unusual or unexpected 'marked' in some way. This tendency is exemplified by such pairs as skid/non-skid, stick/non-stick, U/non-U, and smoking/non-smoking, where the non- form represents the marked case. There is a further way in which language oversimplifies experience by offering a choice between two categories that purport to exhaust all possibilities between them. If you are not a 'hawk' you must be a 'dove', if not a 'hard-liner' a 'soft-liner'.

Where there are categories, there are boundaries between them, and for most people the maintenance of boundaries between their cate-

58

gories seems to be important. Or rather, it would probably be more accurate to say that for everybody it is important to maintain boundaries between some categories in order to give an essential stability to life, but that some people, perhaps because they feel more secure, find it easier to tolerate mixing of categories. The manager of a football club who said, "I don't think you can be a real sportsman with long hair and sideboards", was revealing a great deal about his category 'sportsman', about the category of people he associated with 'long hair and sideboards', and about his inability to mix them.

The categories to be mixed in 'mixed doubles' and 'mixed foursomes' are provided for in the rules of the game. The conditions under which mixing may take place are explicitly laid down, so that boundaries are relaxed under circumstances which do not endanger security. A phrase like, "They're a mixed bunch" does not perhaps conceal much of a threat, unlike 'mixed marriage' or even, in some societies, 'mixed bathing'. Whether the underlying categories are categories of race, colour, religion, sex or age, it may seem important to keep them apart.

3

Earlier in the chapter, it was suggested that we sometimes continue to operate well-established categories despite the need for reappraisal. The categories underlying the phrase 'mixed ability' are a case in point. The word 'able' is variously qualified to give a variety of sub-categories: more able, less able, very able, not very able, well down the ability range, and so on.

The tendency to categorise in terms of simple teachability is further revealed in the assortment of terms used to describe pupils. It is significant that such terms occur in all kinds of school, irrespective of the way in which its pupils have been selected. In grammar schools, terms like "D-stream type/element" or, more euphemistically, the "awkward squad", together with remarks like, "The trouble is they haven't any/many brains", serve to mark off those who fall below expectations. In one direct grant school, which prided itself on the number of Open Awards it gained annually, those who seemed unlikely to gain an acceptable number of O Levels at the end of four years were relegated to what was known variously as 'the sink', 'the drain' or 'the tip'. In other schools there is the kind of labelling that categorises some as 'noddies' or 'thickies', as 'dim' or 'dull' or 'not very bright', together with the inevitable categorisation by reference to IQ—'low IQ', 'not very high IQ', 'he's got a good IQ, he ought to be doing better'.

Liam Hudson claims in his Introduction to "The Ecology of Human Intelligence" that "Quasi-religious conceptions of intelligence are on the wane: the idea of I.Q. as the sign of the mental aristocrat, the member of the Genetic Elect'." But, he continues, "All the same, the notion of mental capacity is still with us, albeit in blurred and more differentiated form."

In "Expectation and Pupil Performance", Douglas Pidgeon discusses the confusion that arises when the word 'intelligence' is used indiscriminately to mean three different things: innate potential, general level of performance, and the results of intelligence tests. Of such tests, especially those supposedly designed to be free "from the handicaps of language", he says "most users believed that they were indeed getting a measure of intelligence that was relatively free from cultural influences and from the difficulties associated with language." Yet, in his contribution to "Intelligence and Cultural Differences", Eells could point to five factors bearing on the level of performance in those tests: genetic potential; environmental factors bearing on development; cultural bias in test items drawn from cultural materials unequally accessible to those being tested; test motivation; and test work habits or test skills. To these may be added a sixth—language, which is not only a factor in its own right, as it bears on the ability of the child to handle the language of the test itself, but enters into, and adds a dimension to, all the other factors.

We have seen how human beings are genetically equipped to learn language, so that even children with mongolism can learn language. But the relationship between this basic human characteristic and the capacity subsequently to develop language to fulfil the demands of formal learning, about which Peter Doughty has more to say in Chapter 7, is not yet fully understood. What is becoming understood, however, is the part played in determining pupil performance by teacher expectation, whether that expectation derives from notions of intelligence, judgements about language, or a combination of both. Such expectations are inevitably transmitted by language, based upon the kind of oversimplifying categorisation represented by a phrase like 'mixed ability'.

FURTHER READING

M. L. Johnson Abercrombie, *The Anatomy of Judgement* (Pelican).

R. Brown, "How shall a thing be called?", in *Language*, ed. R. C. Oldfield and J. C. Marshall (Penguin).

Mary Douglas, *Purity and Danger* (Penguin).

L. Hudson, Introduction to *The Ecology of Human Intelligence*, ed. Hudson (Penguin).

E. Leach, "Animal Categories and Verbal Abuse" in *New Directions in the Study of Language*, ed. E. H. Lenneberg (M.I.T.).

D. Pidgeon, *Expectation and Pupil Performance* (National Foundation for Educational Research).

Five   Language and relationships

1

The two preceding chapters have explored how language is acquired and used in interpreting an individual's experience of the world. Through language, a speaker discriminates one experience from another, classifies and records what he experiences and shapes his understanding of what he has experienced. All this, however, concentrates upon the individual as a user of language, yet;

> ". . . language functions as a link in concerted human activity, as a piece of human behaviour."

In this chapter and the next, therefore, the focus must shift from the individual to society, for what is characteristically 'human' in human behaviour is the use of language to mediate between one individual self and another, and thereby initiate, maintain and regulate relationships. From a linguistic point of view, however, there are two aspects to every relationship, the use of language to make contact with others and the degree to which the social context for the meeting governs its use. Our intuitions make clear to us, however, that what we say does depend upon who we say it to and where we say it, so that once again exploring language has to begin with the familiar. This time, however, the problem is a little more complicated, because the subject involves the speaker's intuitions about society as well as about language.

In Chapter 1, the idea of folk-linguistic was introduced and its power to persuade a speaker that he already knows what he needs to know about language and its function was examined. A similar situation exists in relation to an individual's understanding of society, because a speaker's social experience is as much a part of him as his linguistic experiences, for he has learnt to function as a member of society in the same way as he learnt to use language. In fact, the two go side by side, for the young child learns to relate himself to others in the process of learning to language. Consequently, people possess intuitions about the nature and function of society as deep-rooted and unconscious in their operation as their intuitions about language. They embrace such things as his understanding of words like 'family', 'neighbour', 'community', the social action that is likely to

62

go with membership of a particular social group, an individual's assessment of social class and status, and the very idea of 'society' itself. These intuitions also shape his understanding of the nature and function of institutions like schools and factories and offices and hospitals, so naturally they will play an important part in shaping the teacher's view of being a teacher and how this affects him in his relationships with other members of society. The parallel with folk-linguistic is a close one, for an individual's collective intuitions about society combine to produce a 'folk-social' view of social reality comparable to his folk-linguistic view of linguistic reality.

It has been argued that a man must distance himself from his experience of language if he is to explore its true nature and function, because the limiting effect of folk-linguistic upon his understanding only becomes apparent when it is examined from an objectively linguistic point of view. A corresponding process is necessary in order to see the limiting effects of folk-social, not only upon a man's view of society, but upon his understanding of language itself, because his understanding of *social* reality plays so large a part in shaping his understanding of *linguistic* reality. One of the commonest examples of this is the way in which the response to a speaker's actual pattern of speech is influenced by an assessment of his social status. Another is the degree to which a speaker's choice of language when meeting strangers will be influenced by his reading of the total social situation in which he finds himself. Their dress, manner, the occasion for the meeting, the setting itself, are all used to help him decide what he should say. The professional linguist is free to ignore this fact if he wishes, because there are many problems in the study of language to which it is not relevant, but it cannot be ignored if the focus of linguistic exploration is upon the part played by language in teaching and learning.

If language is "a link in concerted human activity", as Malinowski suggests, then it is necessary to explore the link in order to understand the activity, for society is made up of concerted human activities like teaching and learning, and language makes them possible. Society exists, because men have language; consequently, exploring language cannot stop at the boundaries of language, but must go on to look at the social context which makes the activity of languaging meaningful. It is disconcerting, however, that this argument can be put the other way round. Language is the outcome of "concerted

63

human activity" and its function is to make such activity possible. Language exists, therefore, because the formation of societies requires men to act together: consequently, exploring society should include at some stage an exploration of the linguistic aspects of its structure and processes. Exploring language or exploring society must always, therefore, entail a double focus and the need for this must be stated explicitly, because it is contrary to folk-linguistic ways of thinking about language and folk-social ways of thinking about society.

A fundamental characteristic of these ways of thinking is that they encourage too simple a view of the relationship between language and society. In consequence, many people possess a high resistance to explanations of this relationship that point to the presence of "many layers of meaning". Indeed, human beings going about the everyday business of living and speaking probably could not function effectively unless they were able to interpret social events in a simplified way. There is a limit to the amount and kind of information the brain can make use of when it is engaged in determining actions moment by moment and the time to give detailed thought to how a motor-car works is not when one is negotiating the rush hour traffic in the city centre. When, however, a teacher wants to understand the effect of social processes upon his pupils' use of language, a reliance upon a folk-social understanding of those processes is no longer sufficient to his needs. Moreover, some use of technical language becomes necessary, because common language expressions for social processes embody the underlying folk-social assumptions and attitudes which themselves require investigation. The need to use appropriate technical terms is a continual reminder that there are more 'layers of meaning' to be discovered in the exploration of social relationships than common language expressions can cope with.

2

This chapter is concerned with relationships, because they are the very heart of using language to live. Like language itself, relationships make up so much of the texture of every-day existence that their nature and function are taken for granted. Without thinking about it, an individual will discriminate between close and distant relationships, formal and informal, family, relatives, colleagues,

64

acquaintances, casual contacts, and so on. From his earliest years, working out his relationships to the other human beings has formed an essential part of interpreting his experience of the world. As he grows up, he accumulates experience of contact with others, narrow or wide, according to his social circumstances. He learns the forms that this contact can take, and he develops an intuitive understanding of the ways in which the form of a relationship can govern its possibilities for interaction. He learns that there is an intimacy possible with colleagues through day-to-day contact that is not available with acquaintances. He may go on to learn that a relationship with a doctor or lawyer or a headmaster is a professional relationship and thus has a well-defined purpose that determines what enters into it and what custom or professional decorum excludes. All this is very similar to a speaker's intuitive understanding of how to use language in interaction with others. In fact, the two are intimately associated, for much of the information that an individual draws on in initiating and maintaining relationships he derives from the language others use when in contact with him. If language is "a link in concerted human activity", then it is forged through the making of relationships.

In an advanced industrial society like contemporary Britain, the most obvious feature of relationships is their enormous diversity. It would be a long task to list exhaustively every relationship that an ordinary adult member of the community enters into. Embracing family, a wide circle of friends, work, leisure activities, every-day participation in the life of the community, the use of shops, institutions, and services, it can easily run into three figures. It is as if a man lived within a network of relationships that made up the social context of his actions as a social being. The idea of a network of relationships was used by the British sociologist, Professor J. A. Barnes, and he described it in this way:

> "Each person is, as it were, in touch with a number of other people, some of whom are directly in touch with each other, and some of whom are not. Similarly, each person has a number of friends and these friends have their own friends; some of any one person's friends know each other, others do not. I find it convenient to talk of a social field of this kind as a network. The image I have is of a number of points, some of which are joined by lines. The points of the image are people, or sometimes groups, and the lines indicate which people interact with each other . . . a

65

network of this kind has no external boundary, nor has it any clear-cut internal divisions, for each person sees himself at the centre of a collection of friends."

The image is made stronger if the lines connecting the points of the network are thought of as thick or thin in proportion to the importance of the relationship involved. If an individual is thought of as standing at the centre of a network like this, there will be a cluster of points close to him, representing members of his immediate family, and joined by very thick lines. A little further out will be points representing his immediate circle of friends and those he comes into day-to-day contact with in the course of his work. The lines here will be less thick, but still substantial. Further out will be a large number of points representing all those he knows, or is 'on nodding acquaintance' with in his immediate neighbourhood or community. The lines here will be much thinner, for the relationships involved are limited in range and often no more than a sign of mutual recognition between people in the same locality.

This network of relationships can also be seen as a map of his use of language to live. Every line in it represents the presence of some contact with another human being, or group of human beings. Moreover, it indicates that the contact is reciprocal, for there are always at least two parties to a relationship, and its nature is influenced by both. Each line in the network, however, is also the sign that language has had to be used to initiate, and then maintain, the relationship involved. From a linguistic point of view, therefore, the existence of a relationship is evidence that people are using language for a specific purpose in a particular social context; and that the way in which it is used will be influenced by every party to the relationship. Who people are, what they do together, and for what purpose they do it, provides a mesh which yields the picture of a pattern of relationship or a pattern of language, depending on the angle of one's vision. Looking at it from a social point of view, the observer will see revealed a pattern of individuals acting together socially. It is a picture of some aspect of 'concerted human activity'. Look at the same mesh from a linguistic point of view, however, and what is revealed is a pattern of language in use, the 'links' that make the activity possible.

In this sense, the relationships between teacher and pupil, lecturer and student, teacher and teacher, pupil and pupil, imply the use of

66

language in ways particular to the roles that those words signify. In fact, to use the words 'teacher', 'lecturer', 'pupil', 'student', is to say that the individuals so named are involved in using language for learning. At the same time, these words indicate the part played by the individuals concerned in the social context of the school. The names mark the roles that they perform as members of the social body, school or college, within which they work. To take up a role, then, is to enter into a particular relationship within a particular social context, and the ability to find the language appropriate to it is a basic condition for being able to take it up, or exercise it, successfully. It is for this reason that a detailed examination of what is meant by role must form part of exploring language. It is through the taking up of a role that man's capacity to language engages with his needs as a social being.

As so often in the discussion of language and society, however, there is an initial problem of familiarity to overcome. At first sight, the concept of role and its description may appear to be no more than a very elaborate way of talking about the commonplace. The basic metaphor itself has had a long life in the language and the idea of a man playing many parts is the common property of all who speak the language. People know that they do play many parts, according to their situation in life and circumstances of their day-to-day activities. It is an essential folk-social intuition about how we act in relation to the world about us. People know that those parts are often as different from each other as confident father and diffident employee, amateur yachtsman and national politician, dutiful daughter, fond sister and overbearing wife. Moreover, phrases like 'He wasn't himself at all', 'I'd never have known him for the man who . . .' reflect the underlying social intuition that a man known from one context may appear utterly different when encountered in another. There is more to the question of role, however, than the metaphor of playing a part can convey, and the rest of this chapter is concerned with the nature of the concept and its implications for the understanding of language.

3

The first task is to take a look at the range of roles that an individual possesses. Consider a typical student in his first term at college. At that time he could enter into all of the following roles:

(1) Englishman; Yorkshireman; member of a community
(2) male; son; brother
(3) member of a class; a seminar; a college
(4) voter; traffic offender; Methodist
(5) friend; boyfriend; footballer; photographer.

Obviously, many more items could be added to each heading. Everyone, however, will possess at least one or two entries in each of these five groups: geographical or ethnic; kinship; occupational; public; and personal. It is as if each group provides one of the essential social contexts that go to make up this student's place in his society. Where he comes from, who he is, what he does, his public and his personal relationships, are all facets of his social self, and together they make up the sum of his experience of living in society. Each group, however, has different implications for his use of language. The geographical context yields a mother-tongue, an accent, perhaps a dialect, and pattern of purely local usage. The kinship context will have determined many of his basic attitudes to language, for it is in these roles that he acquired, initially, his 'models of language'. The occupational context at the stage chosen for this student makes a whole new range of demands upon his capacity to use language for learning. Equally, it makes heavy demands upon his ability to use language to take up the new range of roles with which he is faced.

The fourth context, the public, is rather different. In this case, it is as if society were assigning certain rights and privileges to the individual. The most interesting linguistic aspect, therefore, is not so much the language used by the individual in taking up the roles concerned, but the language used to give public expression to the existence of the role. The language of politics, or the language of the law, or the language of religion, constitute a more appropriate focus for linguistic enquiry than the individual's use of that language as a voter, a defendant in court, or a worshipper. His scope for expressing something unique about himself as a person is strictly limited in this context, whereas the personal is precisely that context in which he is called upon most directly to express uniqueness of self through his use of language. It is this context that makes most demand upon his ability to language private needs and hopes and fears.

This student, then, in his first year, enters into a large number of relationships, and in so doing he takes up a wide range of different roles. 'Role', however, is an abstract category, a formal term for describing something that is observable in the normal course of human behaviour. 'Being a son', or 'being a student', are certainly 'roles' in this sense, but they enter into many different relationships. In fact, there is scarcely any aspect of this young man's life that will not be affected by his 'being a son' or 'being a student'. Most obviously, both roles imply a degree of social and economic dependence upon the decisions of others as to what one can do and cannot do. They constrain an individual's independence of action in relation to fundamentals like getting married, having children, taking a job, and so on. In discussing 'role', therefore, it is useful to be able to distinguish the formal category of the role in question, 'being a son' or 'being a student', from any actual pattern of behaviour which occurs as a consequence of its being taken up. The relationship between this student and his father, or his mother, is not, therefore, the 'role' itself, but one particular *realisation* of it. In this case, the role of 'son' is realised in the social context of the intimate family. The importance of this distinction emerges when it becomes necessary to explore the way in which several 'roles' can combine. In fact, one of the most valuable aspects of the concept of 'role' is its power to clarify complex relationships, like teacher and pupil, by discriminating one from the other among the many distinct 'roles' that are involved.

In our day-to-day behaviour, we necessarily realise a large number of roles in different combinations. There is a limit to the number and character, however, that a particular individual will enter into at any one time. For convenience, these can be referred to as his repertoire of roles. At the point in time chosen for this example, his first year at college, all the roles listed above are present in this student's repertoire. Taken together, the roles in his repertoire represent his current experience of relationships, the sum of his present activities as a member of family, community, and society. It makes up the register of possibilities he sees open to him as a social self. Looked at from the linguistic point of view, however, his repertoire represents his current experience of using language '. . . as a link in concerted human activity'. Realising a role, or a combination of roles, in a particular social context like a classroom, is a sociological description of what Professor Firth meant by 'how we use language to live'.

Though it is a handy term for referring to a person's entire current experience of relationships, a 'repertoire' is not to be thought of as an easily distinguishable collection of individual roles, each clearly separated from the others, like the list of parts for Professor Leach's motor-car. Living is a much more complicated matter than engineering and it seldom lends itself to tidy analysis. It is necessary to be content with much less sharply definable categories in the field of social sciences than is customary in the field of physical science. Consequently the fact that, like Professor Barnes' social network, a repertoire "... has no external boundary, nor has it any clear-cut internal divisions" does not detract from its usefulness in discussing patterns of social action.

In particular, a repertoire does not remain unchanged over long periods of time. All the roles that this student acquires as a consequence of living in a particular geographical context may well remain with him throughout his life, even though they are capable of undergoing considerable modification in the course of it. Again, all those that he takes up in the family or kin context remain with him for much of his life, but 'being a son' at age five, age fifteen, and age forty-five involve very different patterns of social action. Moreover, 'being a son' will retain a posthumous relevance, for even after the relationship with parents has been ended by their death, its effects continue to influence the lives of their children. Roles acquired in an occupational context, however, are likely to have a much less pervasive effect upon an individual and their actual number and variety is much more open to change. None of this student's present occupational roles would have been in his repertoire the year before, and they will pass out of it again when he leaves college, to be replaced by a new set associated with the career that he adopts. A person's repertoire, then, includes some roles that always remain his, like 'being a native speaker of English', or 'being male', or 'being a West Indian' and some that remain, but show a pattern of progressive modification in the course of an individual's life, like 'being a son' or 'being a husband'. There are others that remain open to him only for a limited period of time, like 'being a child', or 'being a full-time college student', while others continue to remain a possibility, like 'being a defendant in court' or 'being a boy-friend' or 'being a patient', but may or may not be in his repertoire at any one moment.

The complicating factor in all this is that a person has both a present 'social self' and a 'social history'. His repertoire of roles represents his present social self, but that self is also a product of his social history as an individual. All his current relationships realise a combination of the roles in his repertoire, but they are also a reflection of his cumulative experience of relationships, the sum of what he has learnt through acting socially as a member of a family, a community and a society. At the same time, his repertoire is also a reflection of how successfully he has learnt to use language for entering into and monitoring relationships. Just as the range of roles it contains represents his cumulative experience of relationships, so, from a linguistic point of view, that range represents the scope of his competence for languaging social action.

As ordinary human beings, however, our habit is to focus upon an individual's present social self, rather than see him as a product of a particular social history. If a student has difficulty in realising the role of 'student', therefore, we normally focus upon those present difficulties and overlook the experience of relationships that might have created them. In the context of formal learning, the teacher's expectations about 'being a student' are critical, for they represent a strongly developed idea of the kind of behaviour that ought to occur. In particular, they will include expectations about the *linguistic* behaviour that the teacher believes appropriate to the role of 'student' but he will also have similar expectations about the linguistic behaviour that is appropriate to the other relevant roles of 'teacher' and 'learner'. These expectations, however, may well overlook an individual student's 'history', yet it is precisely his 'history' that will determine whether or not he can, in fact, realise the roles of 'student' and 'learner' in the way in which his teachers expect. In particular, past experience in such roles as 'school-boy', 'junior school pupil', 'adolescent', Leaving Certificate or 'A-Level candidate', influence his ability to find the language for meeting the linguistic demands of 'student' and 'learner' when he does eventually arrive at college.

To sum up, a pupil or student brings his past experience of 'being a learner' to each new stage of his progress through the educational system, and consequently his ability to realise any of the roles that the system requires of him depends upon his cumulative history as a 'learner'. From a linguistic point of view, this is to say that 'pupil' or 'student' is a product of a cumulative experience of learning

71

situations: the ability to find the language for learning demanded by each new situation, therefore, will depend upon past success in being able to take up the roles of 'pupil' and 'learner'.

4

There is an enormous literature on the subject of role and this chapter aims at doing no more than point out the importance of the concept, for the exploration of language and for the understanding of relationships between teachers and pupils. Moreover, there are several different ways of describing role. Each seems to add something to the understanding of its nature and function as a key factor in social processes, yet no one explanation seems adequate to account for all its aspects. No Newton or Darwin has yet appeared to produce a single satisfactory theory that will weld into one the current diversity. The immensity of the task has been put most sharply by Konrad Lorenz in his introduction to *On Aggression*:

> "It is almost impossible to portray in words the functioning of a system in which every part is related to every other in such a way that each has a causal influence on the other.... Unless one understands the elements of a complete system as a whole, one cannot understand them at all. The more complex the structure of a system is, the greater this difficulty becomes.... Unfortunately, the working structure of the instinctive and culturally-acquired patterns of behaviour which make up the social life of man, seems to be one of the most complicated systems we know on this earth."

It is not surprising, therefore, that present understanding is partial and incomplete, but even so it is sufficiently developed to enable us to transcend the limitations of a merely folk-social view of social relationships.

Of these various ways of describing role, two are particularly important for the present context and a little will be said about each in turn to indicate how they bear upon the problems of teaching and learning. One approach is to think of role from the point of view of the person who takes it up. This is to see the individual as the player of a part and the emphasis falls upon the fact that every person acts out a situation according to the way in which he sees himself involved in it. The other is to see a role as a point in a network of relationships, a focus for a particular combination of rights and obligations that exist between one individual, or group of individuals, and another. In this sense, taking up a role defines an individual's scope for social action, because it limits and controls his contact with others. Both ways of looking at social relationships have had a long history, but the former is more readily recognisable as it has entered the language and provides a whole range of expression for talking about people's relationships with each other.

Unfortunately, in recent years, the idea of 'playing a part' has come to be set in opposition to 'being yourself': and playing a part is regarded as an insincere expression of self. Interestingly enough, this view of role seems very prevalent amongst teachers, especially teachers of younger pupils. It is as though they believe there is a 'true self' that they can help develop, and set in opposition to the taking up of a number of 'social selves'. What has happened is an excellent demonstration of the way in which a particular value comes to inhere in particular words and phrases. In earlier centuries, the idea of a man playing many parts was a powerful and effective way of pointing to an inescapable aspect of the human condition, for no man is the same person throughout his life, because age and experience leave their marks upon the self. To us, "You're just playing a part", "You can see he's only putting it on", "That's not his real self", "That's not the sort of person he really is", show how the language has been modified by the Romantic idea of a self which was somehow discoverable behind, or beneath, all the selves that a man revealed in his day-to-day behaviour.

When we think of 'playing a part', it has become synonymous in our minds with 'putting it on', a necessarily insincere expression of self in social action. Consequently, 'playing a part' is automatically assumed to be a conscious and deliberate act, an expression of calculated intent, whereas 'being yourself' is supposed to be the person that you are when you are not thinking consciously about being anybody. 'Playing a part', however, in the sense of taking up a role, is no more a necessarily deliberate and conscious act than 'speaking a language'. There are, indeed, times when an individual can be consciously aware both of 'playing a part' and of 'speaking a language', but these activities are normally and properly carried on by mental processes that remain unconscious. It is significant,

73

however, that an individual most often becomes conscious of 'speaking a language' when he is most conscious of 'playing a part'. We 'look to our manners' and 'choose our words with care' in social contexts that feel awkwardly unfamiliar or where we feel unsure of what the other participants expect of us.

There are three aspects of role as the playing of a part that need a brief separate examination:

(1) the way in which a role is regarded by the one who takes it up;
(2) the social behaviour that others think appropriate to it; and
(3) the behaviour that they expect to see.

(1) The action a person takes in any social context follows from his understanding of the scope and limits of the role required of him: he will behave as a pupil, or student, or a teacher, according to his view of what is appropriate to playing the part. An adolescent who accepts that 'being a pupil' is an appropriate role for him will react to school in a very different way from one who regards it as something imposed upon him by forces outside his control. The former comes to the role of 'pupil', knowing that 'being a pupil' carries with it the right to exercise control over his actions. He knows that 'being a pupil' is a necessary preliminary step towards the goal of 'being a doctor/engineer/accountant' or whatever he wants to do. At home, in his family, amongst his friends, and for his immediate community, 'being a school-boy' is a very acceptable part for him to play. In other words, for him 'school' is an integral element in his world, and his view of the role of pupil is intimately influenced by the fact.

In contrast, the other adolescent regards the role of 'pupil' as beyond his comprehension. It seems divorced from the interests and objectives of his life outside school, because there seems to be nothing in that life to which he can relate it. The ultimate goal of 'being a pupil' does not help, because it is connected to a pattern of deferred achievement that is also outside his experience. His teachers will seem remote and unfamiliar, because their actions express a view of their role that he cannot interpret. In particular, their ways of speaking will seem arbitrary, and frequently incomprehensible, especially where the use of language for exercising control over him is concerned. Far from supporting him, the

74

attitude to 'being a school-boy' amongst his family and friends may well put him at risk. In terms of his understanding of the role of 'pupil', the demands of school and the claims of home prove impossible to integrate into one coherent view of what behaviour would be appropriate to its exercise. In particular, the demands of language for learning do not relate to any of the ways of speaking he is called upon to use in the rest of his life outside school.

Whereas one adolescent sees 'being a pupil' as a fully satisfactory role, willingly accepted, the other sees it as a role he has to take up with little hope of ever being able to play the part it requires to the satisfaction of those who create the setting for its exercise.

This example illustrates the fact that 'speaking the part' is a vital factor in an individual's estimate as to whether or not he can 'play the part' successfully. The different attitudes of those two adolescents towards the role of 'pupil' stem, ultimately, from their different estimates of the possibility of their finding the language that they need to 'play the part' of pupil. The pupil from the middle-class home finds familiar patterns of language used by his teachers, for instruction and for control, because there is continuity between home and school. He is accustomed to ask and answer questions of a genuinely exploratory kind and to make a deliberate attempt to be explicit about his needs and actions. He has met, at home, phrases like "Don't you think you ought to get the work done?", "You will return the book, won't you?", "I'd rather you didn't do that", whereas the other is more likely to have met phrases like "stop it, or else", "Get it done", or "Take that". The child's model for regulatory language, therefore, will have a decisive effect upon his understanding of what words imply what kinds of control over him, and this will contribute to his later view of his role as 'pupil'. Unless he is easy in his interpretation of the patterns of verbal control that he meets with in the school context, the role of 'pupil' will simply seem much too difficult and he will contract out by becoming 'apathetic' or 'difficult'.

(2) A key element in the idea of role as the 'playing of a part' is what the audience understand by it. In this context, 'audience' is a very broad term. It can mean a social group as small and local as a family, or a close circle of friends, or a peer group; it can

mean 'school', or the local neighbourhood, or the wider community of village or town; or it can mean 'society at large', 'they', 'the Establishment' 'all adults', 'grown-ups' and so on. In general, the attitude of the audience reflects those commonly received ideas about roles which express the folk-social view of their exercise. In contemporary British society, judges are expected to be uninfluenced by social or economic considerations and generals to play no part in politics. Husbands are not supposed to beat their wives, nor mothers with young children to go out to work. Students should not criticise the content of courses or their presentation, nor engage in radical political action. Teachers should teach what is obviously useful like 'the 3 R's' or 'O-Level' and see that pupils 'behave themselves'.

A man is always aware of 'audience' when he plays a particular part, but 'audiences' will vary in their power to influence his interpretation of a role. Who a man is, where he lives, what he does, however, determines the range of 'audience' to which he is susceptible. Consequently, in a society as varied as contemporary Britain, wide consensus about what behaviour is appropriate to a particular role will be much rarer than most people realise. Peoples' sense of 'audience' is expressed through the language that they use for evaluating patterns of social action and they have difficulty in conceiving of alternative standards of behaviour, because this language is the only one available to them. In languaging their sense of what is right and proper for the exercise of a particular role, they are languaging a vital part of their understanding of social reality, and the ability to conceive of alternative realities depends upon the ability to find language in which to express them.

(3) Finally, there is the question of the behaviour that people actually expect to see from the exercise of a role. Whereas people believe that judges should *be* impartial, many of them, for particular social reasons, do not expect judges to *act* impartially. Similarly, though husbands should not beat wives, or wives with very young children go out to work, many groups in society expect both things to occur regularly. Students are now expected to dress casually, be promiscuous, take drugs and refuse to give appropriate energy to their academic commitments. In these cases and many similar, the view of a role that people have acquired through growing up with the received ideas about its proper

76

exercise comes into conflict with the playing of the part as they actually observe, or think they observe it.

The language in which teachers talk about teachers and pupils is normally the language that they have developed along with their experience of the role, but it contains much that derives from 'audience' views of the role. Consequently, they describe what they actually expect to see in terms of what they believe they ought to see. Much of the acrimony in current public discussions about teaching and learning, especially discussions about 'progressive methods', arises because the argument is conducted in terms of what a particular 'audience' believes appropriate to the roles of 'teacher', 'pupil', 'child', and so on. The language used in this public discussion is the language through which folk-social views of the roles are expressed.

This question will be pursued in the following chapter, because it involves social *structure*, as well as social relationships, but it is at the root of the tension between what people think appropriate to a role and what behaviour they actually expect to see.

5

Although there is a great deal more to the analysis of role as the playing of a part than this brief sketch can suggest, it has perhaps been sufficient to show that everyday ways of thinking about it are not really adequate to an understanding of its implications for exploring language. The single most important element in a learning situation is the participants' view of what language is appropriate for learning: and the language that they think appropriate to the situation will be determined by the teacher and pupil, lecturer and student, or instructor and apprentice. Approaching this in importance, however, is the participants' view of what rights and obligations the very idea of being a 'pupil' or being a 'teacher' entail. The notion of an individual's rights and obligations in relation to a particular role introduces the alternative view of role that was mentioned earlier. If the essence of the first view is that the individual plays a particular part in a particular social context, then the essence of the second is that there is a contractual basis to all relationships. From this alternative point of view, taking up a role is equivalent to taking up certain rights and assuming the corresponding obligations. Moreover, this process is reciprocal, for all the parties to the relationship not only take up rights in relation to each other, but also assume an equivalent pattern of obligations. The metaphor changes from the theatre to the court of law.

The next stage is to consider how an individual stands in relation to these rights and obligations. Broadly, there is a distinction between those which follow from a role that he cannot avoid, like 'being a speaker of English', 'being a son', 'being a negro', and those that are a consequence of a role that he has taken up of his own accord, like 'student', 'teacher' or 'headmaster'. Obviously, the element of deliberate personal decision may vary. The eldest son may have little option about 'going into the business'; many students find themselves students as a consequence of an educational conveyor belt rather than their own deliberate choice. However, there is an important distinction between the roles which result from being born 'the man you are', in a particular place and at a particular time, and those that are taken up in the ordinary course of day-to-day living. At one extreme, a person *is* male or female, son or daughter, black or white; at the other, he *becomes* a teacher, a headmaster, a rate-payer, a sportsman. What he *is* will influence his behaviour at every point, but what he *becomes* may touch only one small area of his life. Banton distinguishes these two types of role by calling those that enter into all situations BASIC and those that are more or less limited to a specific context INDEPENDENT. These are not two water-tight compartments, however, but rather the opposite ends of a con-tinuous line along which all the roles that a man takes up could be plotted, from most basic to most independent, according to the degree of freedom he has in taking them up.

The most basic of roles are normally the product of combining age, ties of kinship, sex, and ethnic factors. Close to this are such roles as husband or wife, parent, member of a religious faith. There are, besides, roles that operate like basic roles in that they are virtually inescapable for the individual concerned, and do affect his life at very many points, although on the surface they appear to be more like independent roles. One of the most obvious is 'pupil'. In the vast majority of cases, in our society, 'being a pupil' from the age of five to fifteen is as inescapable a consequence of being born as 'being male' or 'being a son'. This is important, from a linguistic point of view, because the rights and obligations attaching to basic roles are much more likely to be taken for granted, to be implicit in the

78

culture, than explicitly stated and discussed objectively in relation to the responsibilities and privileges of the job concerned. Hence, the language in which pupils' rights and obligations are discussed is likely to be language that directly expresses the folk-social understanding of the role. An objective and rational discussion of the role, therefore, will be much more difficult to set up than it would be if the role of 'pupil' were looked upon as truly 'independent', like the role of 'lecturer' or 'scientist'.

Independent roles, on the other hand, are the product of highly circumscribed situations, and the pattern of rights and obligations that they entail carries little, if at all, beyond the social context in which the role functions. In a contemporary industrial society, the vast majority of ordinary jobs are of this kind, so much so that there is a tendency to think that all jobs should be as self-contained as the majority. This is reflected in popular resistance to the idea that a company should interview a prospective manager's wife, or a local political party the wife of a prospective candidate. This last example, however, points to the fact that there are roles remaining in our society which oblige those who take them up, no matter how voluntarily, to live their lives according to public notions of what is appropriate to the role concerned. To these, Banton has given the name of GENERAL. The most obvious examples are provided by senior representatives of the older professions, like Admirals, Queen's Counsel and Bishops. In these cases, a man's occupation determines, in almost all situations, how others expect him to behave. Much less obviously, the role of 'grammar school boy' has something of the same consequences for the individual, because the 'grammar school' still retains much prestige as a focus of local pride in many communities. A sure sign that this is the case can be found by looking at the reasons advanced in the correspondence columns of the local press for the retention of a clearly distinguishable grammar school uniform. It is to help the community to assess whether or not its wearer behaves according to their expectations for the role of 'grammar school-boy'.

In this context, 'teacher' is, at present, a highly ambivalent role. For many people, 'being a teacher' is incompatible with 'being promiscuous', 'being politically radical', 'being an unbeliever'. For them, it is still clearly a general role. For others, however, 'being a teacher' is like 'being a draughtsman' or 'being a car-salesman', for it is an independent role, a job like any other, and the private life of the person concerned is only relevant insofar as it interferes with the job being properly done. The effect of this ambivalence in society itself is reflected in the individual teacher's understanding of what rights and obligations fall upon him in consequence of taking it up. This has one major consequence in the field of language. If a teacher thinks of his role in *general* terms, rather than *independent*, he is likely to accept current cultural ideas about what his obligations are. One of the most important of these ideas is that the teacher's task is to civilise the majority through teaching them 'the proper use of the English language'. The whole area of language in the school context then becomes mixed up with deeply held feelings about what is right or wrong with the lives of the pupils in question.

FURTHER READING

M. Banton, *Roles* (Tavistock Publications).

P. L. Berger, *Invitation to Sociology* (Penguin).

J. R. Firth, "Personality and Language in Society", in *Papers in Linguistics, 1934–1951* (O.U.P.).

R. Frankenberg, *Communities in Britain*, Chapters 9 and 10 (Penguin).

C. Hannam, P. Smyth and N. Stephenson, *Young teachers and reluctant learners*, Chapter 3 (Penguin).

W. J. H. Sprott, *Human Groups* (Penguin).

Six   Language and society

1

The last chapter focused upon the part played by language in enabling people to make relationships, and, consequently, it was concerned with relationships from the point of view of the individuals who form them, rather than with the settings in which they occur. In this chapter, therefore, the focus shifts from the roles people take up to the social contexts which bring them into being.

One way of looking at the idea of role, employed in Chapter 5, was to see it as the playing of a part, but it is possible to reverse the analogy and look at a play as the acting out of a particular pattern of relationships. Each character is then seen in terms of a particular combination of roles like 'son', 'nephew', 'disappointed heir', 'prince', 'melancholic', or 'elder', 'courtier', 'politician', 'father'. The action of the play presents the realisation of these roles through particular sequences of interaction, staged in a number of recognisable settings like 'council chamber', 'bedroom', 'deck of a ship'. The average audience, however, focuses upon the interaction and is unconscious of any response to the relationship between interaction and setting. This is similar to our normal behaviour as members of society. We get on with being members of a family, a business, a school, a community and so on, without reflecting at all closely upon the social setting in which our actions take place. This is because we are involved in being players to the audience of others and of being, in turn, an audience for their actions.

In the theatre, especially with an audience accustomed to naturalistic conventions of acting and presentation, people expect there to be a close parallel between inter-action presented in the play and the social behaviour of ordinary people in ordinary situations. They judge the validity of interaction in the theatre, therefore, against their own experience of interaction in the world outside it. In doing so, they seldom take into account the conventions of the theatre: the fact that the audience normally sit in the dark, looking into a brightly lit area; that the actors wear costumes, use make-up, and employ movements, gestures, and styles of delivery that exist only in the context of the theatre: that plays can be in high style or low, verse or prose, or a mixture of both: that plays happen because there

81

are people to finance the players, and pay for the theatre in which they perform. Similarly, a man tends to evaluate the social action in which he takes part, or which comes to his notice, without thinking directly about such things as the relevance of the physical setting to the action; the movement, dress, gesture, and so on of the participants; or any other aspect of the total social context in which the action takes place. Just as in the theatre, however, 'willing suspension of disbelief' remains a suspension only, the parallel 'necessary operational focus upon the action of others' does not leave a man unaware that there *is* a social context and that it does affect the action that takes place within it.

This awareness is often verbalised in remarks like "Just what you'd expect, coming from a background like that", or "Those are impossible conditions to work in" or "Curious way to go on, but then they're from the North/South/East/West". Intuitively, on reflection, we do make this kind of relation between actions and their context, and the resulting body of accumulated experience forms part of an individual's view of social reality. In turning to the exploration of the part played by language in society, then, it is very necessary to acquire an explicit understanding of the nature and function of social context, because the bias in our intuitive understanding of language leads us so readily to an exclusive focus upon it as an extension of human personality. The importance of society as the theatre for social action is consequently under-emphasised and the effect of social circumstances upon the use of language for living fails to receive due weight. The most serious consequence of this attitude, as far as the teacher is concerned, is that it leads to a picture of language in use in which the speaker's freedom to choose what he wants to say is emphasised, rather than the way in which social context has a constraining effect upon that freedom.

Broadly, the constraints upon what we say and the way in which we say it are social in origin. The idea that language need only be 'appropriate' because 'they' want it to be appeals to some teachers of English and leads them to think that 'appropriateness' is something *imposed* upon the 'natural', 'spontaneous', 'imaginative' use of language by the demands of a society hostile to 'the very culture of the feelings". In effect, however, 'appropriateness' is merely one way of describing the fact that any use of language, however 'spontaneous' or 'imaginative' is relatable to a particular *social* context,

82

because language only occurs within the framework of 'society'. Like 'language', 'society' is one of those words which seems to refer to a vague abstraction, yet everyday usage is full of phrases which reveal an individual awareness of those shaping forces that bear upon us as members of a society. The ubiquitous 'They' who should 'do something about it', is a form of reference to powers or forces in society that almost everyone finds himself using at some time or other. Though the reference seems to be personal, its linguistic form invariably indicates that, whoever 'They' are, the speaker does not see himself entering into a relationship with 'Them'. The grammatical contrast is with the use of 'we', as in phrases like "People like us", "We can't let it happen", "It's up to us to do something about it". These phrases recognise the possibility of collective action, but they refer to a pattern of relationships embracing the 'we' that speaks, and not to the social context in which the 'we' has to act. "It's up to us" expresses a folk-social intuition about social relationships, whereas "They ought to do something about it" expresses an intuition about the organisation of power within society as a whole.

Our view of social reality does incorporate a basic idea of 'society', just as our view of linguistic reality incorporates a basic idea of 'language'. Whatever 'society' and 'language' may actually be, our understanding of social and linguistic reality makes us readily aware that both of them act upon the life of every individual in ways which are decisive and inescapable. W. J. H. Sprott, the social psychologist, put this very well when he says that "it is nonesensical . . .

> to say that we have a direct acquaintance with society. We do not. We have a direct acquaintance only with people interacting, i.e. the elements of which society, insofar as it exists at all, is constituted. So I say that society is in some sense a figment of the imagination. But we do have in our minds models of the society in which we live."

In terms of this quotation, a speaker does not have a 'direct acquaintance' with 'language' any more than he does with 'society'. What he actually experiences are the linguistic manifestations of relationships, for he can only have a 'direct acquaintance' with language in use, which is the linguistic realisation of a relationship and not 'language' itself. Even though 'language' is therefore as much a 'figment of the imagination' as 'society', exploring language

83

exploits the fact that a speaker's linguistic intuitions persuade him that language not only exists but also shapes his thoughts and actions. When, therefore, that exploration extends to 'society', it is important to appreciate that "... we do have in our minds models of the society in which we live" because similar models have already been met in the process of exploring language.

These "models of society" reveal themselves in reference to 'the family', 'the middle class', 'industry', 'the government', 'law and order', 'public morality' 'or 'comprehensive education'. The interesting thing about these words and phrases is the way in which they are used as the subjects of sentences. "The family must defend itself against its detractors": "Law and order demands heavier sentences": "Comprehensive education sweeps away traditional standards of excellence." The language allows people to speak about these abstractions as though they were objects that existed, just as it allows the use of the word 'language' for the same sort of purpose. Such phrases represent a much more abstract view of social reality than most of the people who regularly use them are willing to accept if they meet it in the literature of the social sciences.

There are three major aspects of 'society' that are particularly relevant to the exploration of language: the way in which people come together into recognisable social groups; the powers and agencies, social, economic, political and moral, that act through them; and the means by which a newcomer can learn how to be a member of 'society'. There is one process, however, that plays a crucial part in every aspect of 'society', the process of *interaction*: for "We have direct acquaintance only with people interacting". In looking at relationships as the playing of a part or the taking up of particular clusters of rights and obligations in the previous chapter, the focus had to be upon the individual person who made relationships, but it always takes two, at least, to make a relationship, and what any party to a relationship does must affect every other party. Relationships, therefore are a matter of 'interaction' rather than 'action', because everyone engaged in a particular social context will affect, and be affected by, everyone else in the same context. In fact, social action is synonymous with interaction, because all social action involves contact with other people.

Applied to the class-room, this means that teacher and student do not function independently of each other. How the teacher teaches is constrained by how the students learn, and how the students learn is constrained by how the teacher teaches. This may seem self-evident, but usually discussions about teaching and learning are carried on in terms of *what* is to be taught and learnt, rather than *how* the relationship between teacher and student can best enable learning and teaching to take place. The common language for comment on teaching and learning, however, virtually ignores the interaction involved. Student performance is discussed in terms of 'interest' or 'apathy', 'intelligence' or 'dimness', as though these elements appear independently of any action on the part of the teacher.

If social behaviour is a matter of 'interaction', rather than simply of 'action', then a crucial element in interaction must be language, because people will be as much affected by what is said on any occasion as by what is done. How an individual uses language, therefore, not only depends upon who he is, where he is, and what relationship holds between him and the others concerned at the moment of speaking, but also upon the linguistic pattern of the interaction involved. His own choice of language will be shaped by all that is said in the course of the interaction: how it was initiated, who says what, in what manner, and to whom. As Douglas Barnes has shown, a teacher's questions can determine the linguistic pattern of the interaction to such an extent that students end up in a position where they can say only what he wants them to say.

Linguistically, interaction involves everyone concerned in a continuous process of reassessment in order to be able to select the language that most readily fits its changing needs as it progresses. (See Chapter 8.) Where the direction of work is wholly determined by the exposition and questions of the teacher, the linguistic pattern of the interaction ensures that a student's choice of language for learning is severely restricted. He is only free to learn so long as he can use the language for learning which intermeshes with his teacher's choice of language for teaching.

2

The first step in exploring social context is to see that the actual fabric of society is made up of innumerable groups of individual men and women, held together by links which arise out of their involvement in 'concerted human activity'. These social groups provide the individual with his theatre for social action: they are the immediate social context for the roles that he has to take up. In the last chapter, the enormous diversity of a contemporary industrial society, like Britain, was related to the multiplicity of different roles that its members have to assume in the course of their day-to-day lives. It is not surprising, therefore, to find that this enormous diversity also finds expression in the range, shape, size and function of the social groups which such a society contains. In exploring the diversity of roles, it was useful to consider them in relation to five types of social context (see p. 68): these five can also be used to examine the diversity of social groups as the group provides the local context for the role. This is not the place for an exhaustive analysis of the social group, however, and what follows is merely a brief illustration of the part played by language in enabling such a diversity of social groups to come into being and to achieve individual identity.

The first of the five types of context, the GEOGRAPHICAL, embraces those groups which come into being through the forces of proximity or locality. While they vary greatly in scale, from a group which includes all those who speak the same mother-tongue, to one which embraces only those who live in the same street, or come from one district of a city, or one village, the key factor in their existence is that a man becomes a member of the group concerned simply through residence. The interaction that he is drawn into as a consequence of his membership of such a group arises out of *where* he is, rather than *who* he is, or *what* he does. On the other hand, membership of groups within the second type of context, the FAMILIAL, is determined by *who* a man is: he cannot choose family or kin, or the styles of interaction that they demand of him. Like speaking a mother-tongue, membership of a family is a life-long matter, whatever modifications occur as a man grows up. Again, like his language, the effect of belonging to a particular family will make itself felt in every area of a man's life. The racial or ethnic group to which he belongs, however, results from a combination of these first two types. This illustrates the fact that a particular social group may represent the co-existence of more than one type of social context, just as the part a man plays in a particular context may represent a combination of roles.

The most notable feature about the OCCUPATIONAL context is the number of different groups that it can provide for any one individual, their range and diversity, and their comparative lack of permanence as against those to be found within the first two. For example, pupils gathered together to be taught form a social group and a teacher becomes a member of every group that he teaches: 'the Staff' constitutes another group, which may, in fact, contain within it smaller groups, such as younger/older staff, or men/women staff, or academic/craft staff. Professional associations like the N.U.T., the Science Masters Association, or the National Association for the Teaching of English provide him with a third variety. Notice that the school will contain many social groups, however, to which he does not himself belong, but which he will recognise as having a distinct identity: these would include all the classes that he does not himself teach, every class considered as a 'social' group; groups created by the school's organisation like the year group, streams, sets, juniors and seniors, or by its authority structure like monitors, house captains, and prefects.

Consider the following examples: 'the first year', 'the fourth form', 'the O-Levels', 'the slow stream', 'the Physics Department', 'the Art class', 'the games people', 'the second XI', 'the early leavers'. In every case a noun is used, preceded by 'the', to name a collection of individuals within the school. This frame (the + noun) can obviously be used to do all the things that nouns can do in the grammar of the language, and is thus the most direct way in which the independent existence of a social group can be recognised. Moreover, we learn what nouns are in the process of learning our language, so that when we are presented with the form 'the + noun', we are ready to make all kinds of assumptions about whatever it is being used for. The most important of these is that we have learnt to treat anything occurring in this form as though it could actually exist *per se*, so that 'the fourth form' or 'the second XI' comes to be discussed as though it could exist apart from the collection of individuals gathered together under that label.

The average pupil belongs to a continually changing cluster of groups within the school. He may move up the school with the same people, so that his class continues to form one such group, but the fact that it changes from second year to third year, and from third to fourth, means that he will inevitably be a member of at least one

87

new social group each year. If this seems a trivial point, it should be remembered that many people in the school think of pupils, not as members of 4N, but as members of 'the fourth year' so that they will have a particular set of expectations about the behaviour appropriate to it.

Membership of the groups which arise out of the fourth type of social context, the PUBLIC, will usually have as local an effect upon a man's life as his membership of OCCUPATIONAL groups. In some cases, however, like being in prison or in hospital, for a brief period, membership of a PUBLIC group will completely dominate his existence. Only quite exceptionally does this ever occur for any length of time, as with the life sentence or the incurable mental disorder. Another marked feature of the PUBLIC group is the very wide range in the degree of involvement that membership of them entails. Groups like 'the ratepayers of Dunchester' or 'the voters of Brasingbury' normally demand little of their members, whereas 'first offenders', 'casualties', 'the Church', may demand total involvement. On the other hand, the fifth type of context, the PERSONAL, only really exists when individuals deliberately choose to come together to share common interests. Groups of close friends represent this deliberate and voluntary element particularly well, as do the innumerable social and sporting clubs that our society produces. What this last type also illustrates very clearly is the degree to which the cohesion of a group depends upon the shared 'history' of its members. Full membership of the group can only be achieved by learning to interpret the patterns of language in use that arise from this shared 'history'. The difficulty for the newcomer is that so much of the 'meaning' of what its members say derives from this 'history' and is therefore assumed by them to be self-evident.

In spite of their enormous diversity, however, social groups, like roles, do possess some basic features in common. These relate to the way in which groups achieve a recognisable identity and there are three which are fundamental to their very existence:

(1) groups come into being through the regular and frequent interaction of a collection of individuals over an extended period of time;

(2) the pattern of this interaction distinguishes those who enter into it by virtue of its regularity and frequency;

(3) this pattern of interaction is realised through a distinctive pattern of language in use.

At first glance, there may seem to be little difference between the first two features, but consider the following situation. A collection of individuals meet on the station every morning to catch the 8.10 into town: their interaction is regular, frequent, and certainly may extend over a considerable period of time, and thus it can be said to provide the first of the features listed. There is nothing in the situation itself, however, to distinguish or mark out that collection of individuals from any other. If, however, four of these individuals spend the journey every morning playing cards, then the second feature is provided and it would be possible to talk about these four individuals as a social group. Its membership is restricted to the four who play together, its range of action is limited, and its effects upon the lives of its members is very local, but nevertheless it does represent four individuals fulfilling the minimum conditions for becoming a social group. Moreover, it illustrates the degree to which the very existence of such a group depends upon a particular context, because it only comes into being as a result of the four finding themselves on the same train each day. It also points to the fact that this social context will act as a constraint upon the kind of interaction which the members of the group will feel able to enter into. For instance, this context would be unlikely to encourage the discussion of issues that deeply affected the personal beliefs and values of its members.

A school represents a very different kind of social group. The institution exists over an extended period of time and its members are involved in a pattern of regular and frequent interaction. The interaction will certainly distinguish those involved, because it arises out of a specific commitment to teaching and learning; and it will certainly mark them out as members of a particular social group, because its regularity and frequency is what causes them to be teachers and pupils. It is also the case that the interaction in teaching and learning gives rise to distinctive patterns of language in use. The individuals concerned are members of a recognisable social group, however, insofar as the links between them arise in the social context of the school. This example illustrates the obvious point that taking up a particular role implies entering into a particular social group. To say "I'm a teacher", "He's a headmaster", "She's a pupil", is to imply that they are members of at least one recognisable social group, in this case, a school. This last point underlines the fact that the word 'school' is an abstraction which only *exists* insofar as a collection of individuals gather together in one place over a period of time for an agreed purpose and thereby give it identity through their interaction.

3

From a linguistic point of view, however, patterns of interaction involve patterns of language in use; hence the third means by which social groups can create a recognisable identity is through the distinctive way that they use language. The reader will recall the following passage from the last chapter:

> "Who people are, what they do together, and for what purpose they do it, provides a mesh which yields the picture of a pattern of relationships or a pattern of language, depending on the angle of one's vision."
>
> (p. 66)

In that context, both these patterns were being looked at from the point of view of the individual participant to a relationship and the role that he would take up in consequence. In relation to the social group, however, these patterns have to be looked at as a whole and set in contrast to the patterns that distinguish other recognisably distinct groups. John J. Gumperz is one of a group of linguists working in the United States who have given particular attention to the connections between patterns of interaction and patterns of language. He has been particularly interested in the way in which varieties of a language, or sometimes even different languages, when the community is multilingual, can be used for particular purposes within a given community, and thus leads to the emergence of distinctive social groups. He calls the social context for these varieties a 'speech community', which he defines as:

> ". . . any human aggregate characterised by regular and frequent interaction over a significant span of time and set off from other such aggregates by differences in the frequency of the interaction".

Although he was himself particularly interested in variation within large 'aggregates' like the local district, the town or the village, his definition of 'speech community' coincides with the description of

90

the minimum conditions for the existence of a 'social group' that have been used in this chapter. The 'social group' of the sociologist and the 'speech community' of the linguist are thus one and the same thing, because 'social groups' are aggregates of individual human beings who can be distinguished as a collectivity through the patterns of interaction that relate them to each other, and patterns of interaction are necessarily patterns of language in use.

"By their words ye shall know them", therefore, expresses a basic intuition about the organisation of human society. This distinctiveness in the use of language is often immediately apparent, as with the speaking of a particular language like English, or the use of a strongly marked dialect like Tyneside or Brooklyn, or an accent like West Midlands or Mid-West. It can be as clearly revealed in the use of a professional or technical variety like the speech of lawyers or engineers or in a pattern of usage that is closely connected with a particular trade or occupation. The everyday speech of builders, or mechanics, or cloth-workers, or salesmen contains words and phrases that reveal the social group to which their job assigns them.

More often, however, the distinctive ways in which a particular group draws upon the 'meaning potential' of the language does not show itself quite so immediately. Our intuitions pick up and act upon linguistic clues that our conscious awareness of usage would be hard put to distinguish were it challenged to do so. For instance, at the present time, adults think of 'teenagers' as forming in some sense or other a distinctive group in society. Certainly, this is because they recognise particular patterns of dress, attitudes, and styles of public and personal behaviour, but there is also the underlying sense that a 'teenager' does not use language as an adult would in talking about his experience of the world.

A major element in the adolescent's consciousness of 'being a teenager' derives from his awareness that he does share distinctive ways of speaking with people of his own age, however different from him they may be in other respects. Consequently, the adult response to the way in which adolescents express themselves often takes the form of statements like this: "If you ask them what they want, they can't tell you"; "Young people today are so inarticulate"; or "They don't seem to be able to communicate like ordinary human beings". These phrases have something in common with

91

certain wide-spread reactions to the use of a technical language: "If you ask them what it is all about, they can't tell you in plain language"; "Scientists today are so inarticulate"; or "Economists/psychologists/poets don't seem to be able to communicate like ordinary human beings". What both sets of phrases exemplify is the degree to which the interaction particular to one social group gives rise to ways of speaking and writing that act as a barrier to those who are not members of the group. In fact, Professor Mary Douglas's work suggests that these barriers are a necessary consequence of the processes by which human beings can achieve, and then maintain, a collective identity. The social cohesion of a group depends upon all its members being able to take for granted the fact that everyone in the group shares a common 'history'. The teenager's words for praise or blame, the dialect speaker's words for everyday objects and relationships, the economist's terms of enquiry or analysis, act cohesively only because they are known and understood by all the other teenagers, Tynesiders and economists.

There is an important difference, however, between the ways of speaking that arise within a group embracing 'teenagers' and one embracing 'economists'. Consider for a moment how someone outside the group can become acquainted with the linguistic 'meanings' which are bound up with its ways of speaking. Firstly, he needs to gain experience of their use in the social contexts which gave rise to them. He can do this through direct participation in the group itself, thus acquiring the 'history' that provides a 'local habitation and a name' for the way of speaking in question. Alternatively, he can acquire this experience vicariously through studying the 'history' as it appears in speech and writing. Consequently, there is a distinction between linguistic 'meanings' that exist only in the social context of a group as a result of its shared experience, and those that are used by a group to pursue particular enquiries or perform particular operations and thus, by this means, grow to be a cohesive element in the interaction of its members. The language of teenagers is an excellent example of the former, which can be distinguished as *experientially cohesive*, while the language of any professional group exemplifies the latter, which can be called, therefore, *operationally cohesive*. Vicarious acquisition of the language concerned is thus only really possible for language which is *operationally cohesive*.

It is in this sense that the vast majority of pupils learn the language of the economist, the physicist, or the mathematician vicariously, for they are not expected to 'be' economists, physicists or mathematicians in the process of learning it. One of the recurrent themes in recent developments in science teaching, however, is a concern for the creation of situations in the class-room through which the pupil *can* 'experience what it is like to be a scientist'. The specifically linguistic implications of this attempt to create a more 'real' learning situation have been little commented upon, but one effect would certainly be to give the pupil a chance to learn the technical language involved by using it in interaction, and therefore *experientially*, and not merely vicariously through the glosses of the standard text-book.

The difficulty presented by patterns of language in use that only come into being because they are *experientially cohesive* is that their 'meanings' are only available to someone who becomes a member of the group concerned. Consider for example a teacher faced with the ways of speaking that his pupils use because they are 'teenagers', or belong to a local 'gang', or come from a background different from his own. He cannot become acquainted with these ways of speaking, because he cannot qualify for membership of the groups concerned: he is an adult, or he belongs to a different socio-economic group. What he has to do is to treat these ways of speaking as he would a variety of technical language that he had not previously met. Insofar as he is prepared to give sympathetic attention to an unfamiliar technical language, he will be able to follow its 'meaning', but he is never likely to be able to 'use' the language, because he remains outside the field of enquiry concerned. In the same way, when he is faced with language that is experientially cohesive in the talk or work of his pupils and students, sympathetic attention will give him a working understanding of some of it, but he has to recognise that he can never 'be at home with it', because he can never be a member of the social group that gives rise to it.

The final burden of this argument is that the teacher may well be unaware of the degree to which his own use of language in the class-room is influenced by his membership of social groups to which his pupils do not have access. In particular, it has to be remembered that 'social class' is one kind of social group. If the population of

Britain is thought of in terms of a single broad division into Middle Class and Working Class, the former accounts for 30% of the total and latter 70%. By far the largest percentage of teachers of all kinds are drawn from the Middle Class with the result that most teachers are teaching pupils who are members of a key social group to which they themselves do not belong. The distinctive language habits of social groups *other* than those to which they themselves belong should, therefore, be a major professional concern of all teachers. In particular, teachers need to be aware of patterns of language in use where they are experientially cohesive in the life of a group, especially where they themselves are members of that group and their pupils are not.

4

Just as each social group provides the context for the taking up of particular roles so 'social structure' provides a social context for each group. The very idea of 'social structure', however, seems so remote from day-to-day living that it is difficult for many people to see how it relates to their experience of actual relationships and situations. It has already been suggested, however, that strong intuitions about 'social structure' are developed as a consequence of growing up as members of a society, just as strong intuitions about the nature and function of language are developed as a consequence of learning to speak a language. Each man's view of social reality thus represents his understanding of 'social structure', just as his view of linguistic reality represents his understanding of 'language'. A further quotation from W. J. H. Sprott puts the position very clearly:

> "If some foreigner asks questions about your society . . . you have some sort of model of the society with its political system, economic system, legal system, religious system, class system and so on. . . ."

which you can draw upon to answer him. The language is full of phrases which refer to the workings of 'society' and thus reflect the underlying presence of these models: 'A poor political system that cannot produce a stable government", "The difficulties of running a mixed economy", "The decline of the churches in this century" are representative examples. In the last two cases, the actual words used are, in fact, synonyms for 'economic system' and 'religious' system', for they refer to the way in which the economic or religious life of a society can be seen to be organised as a whole'

"The political system" or "The economic system" is as much a "figment of the imagination" as the idea of 'society' itself, but these phrases are a necessary way of referring to large areas of collective action within a society. There is, however, always the danger that the name will come to be used in such a way as to suggest that the speaker believes in the actual physical existence of the 'figment' in question. 'Systems' are then discussed without sufficient attention to the fact that they are merely a useful collective label for all the interaction that arises from the pursuit of a particular range of activities. The result is likely to be an account of 'social structure' that is much too neat and tidy for the 'messiness' of actual human behaviour.

In any enquiry, linguistic or social, the temptation to treat the terms used in the enquiry as though they were more real than the subject matter is always very strong. The real complexity of events is bent to fit categories of the analysis and the investigator ends up by attaching more importance to the maintenance of his pure categories than to recording and evaluating the behaviour that actually happens. Like role repertoire, introduced in the previous chapter (p. 69), categories used for the analysis of 'social structure' need to be undetermined, so that justice can be done to the fact that human behaviour involves one thing leading to another as much as the setting up and maintaining strong boundaries between one thing and another. This is not just a matter of theoretical interest to those who wish to study 'social structure', however: treating social systems as though they were real, in the normal course of living, can have very serious practical consequences. Consider what happens when a school is thought about as 'The School', an entity existing independently of teachers and pupils and bricks and mortar. Attention is focused upon "what is right" for "The School", what behaviour "The School" demands, even what is appropriate to "The honour of The School". To take an actual example, it could mean that the most suitable examination for the majority of pupils is not available, because "the examination is not one with which the school should be associated". So the needs of "The School" are given precedence over the needs of the pupils: the examination is not available because "The School" does not approve of it; certain activities or

95

careers or jobs are discouraged, because they conflict with "the traditions of the School"; the writ of "The School" is taken to run wherever pupils wear its insignia. "The School" is being treated as a social system with a life and identity of its own, but it is being given that life and identity as a thing apart from the many and complex patterns of interaction that join together all the people involved in it at any one time.

The effects of such a situation are particularly important from the linguistic point of view: just as social systems and social groups only 'exist' insofar as they represent the interaction of particular collections of individuals, so 'language' only exists insofar as its 'elements and structures' are realised through the speech and writing of particular individuals. If, however, a line of argument is used that turns social systems and social groups into actual entities like 'The School', then the focus of exploring language is moved away from "people interacting" towards the linguistic needs and demands of such abstractions as 'Industry', 'Administration', 'Education', and it becomes much more difficult to show how language functions socially, because the context for that function *must* be "people interacting".

While the scope of this book does not permit a detailed exploration of language in relation to 'social structure', the exploration of language cannot afford to ignore it. From a linguistic point of view, it is convenient to be able to talk about this relationship by using a small number of categories which indicate very large areas of "concerted human activity". In pursuing a similar discussion, the American sociologist, William Labov, whose work is referred to in Chapter 10, made use of four such categories of 'social structure' which he borrowed from his fellow American sociologist, Talcott Parsons. They were:

    (1) the kinship system
    (2) socio-economic stratification
    (3) the power system
    (4) systems of value integration.

Each of these four categories outlines the social context for a very complex pattern of relationships, and in so doing, defines the areas within which the use of language as a 'link in concerted human activity' will show interesting differences.

96

The kinship system involves all those relationships that arise from membership of a particular family. It is the social system by means of which new members of society are initiated into its culture and the system through which the young child learns language. Mother tongue, dialect and accent are thus determined by membership of a particular family, and so is the ethnic group to which a person belongs. This is particularly important linguistically, should the mother tongue of the ethnic group be different from the language of the surrounding society of which it is a member. This is the case with Urdu-speaking Pakistanis in Britain, or Indians whose mother tongue is Hindu or Gujerati. One result of this is that members of the group will often use a different language, rather than different varieties of the same language, for different kinds of interaction. Within the social context of the kinship system, therefore, the choice of a way of speaking is determined not so much by *what* a man does, as by *who* he is.

There is an interesting overlap here with the second of these four categories, the SOCIO/ECONOMIC, for this condition is reversed and *what* a man does is the major shaping factor in his use of language. If, however, one says "He's a policeman" or "He's a teacher", there is one sense in which it is like saying "He's an adolescent" or "He's a forge press operative", because the phrases refer both to *who* a man is and *what* he does. From a linguistic point of view, therefore, social groups like policemen or teachers develop characteristic ways of speaking of two distinct kinds. There is a 'language of the trade' which may be a technical language, or a professional short-hand for the discussion of day-to-day problems, or a public language through which these problems can be explored with anyone else in the same field: and there is an *argot*, a way of speaking which is full of meanings and references and implications available only to those who are members of the group concerned. An argot, therefore, is always the product of *experiential cohesion*. Two well-known, extreme examples are the rhyming slang of London cockneys and the original 'thieves argot' of Marseilles. Insofar as the cohesion of such a group is experiential, it can be said to be functioning within the social context of the kinship system, because its identity is achieved through the building up of a history of shared meanings. Like the private linguistic world of a family, the *argot* that results is inaccessible to those who 'do not have the lingo', because so much 'meaning potential' remains implicit and is not realised in the actual

97

pattern of 'elements and structure' that go to make up the uttterances involved.

The linguistic importance of the second category of social context, the SOCIO/ECONOMIC, is the degree to which it is responsible for the enormous diversity of ways of speaking that arise in a complex industrial society like Britain. Membership of the social groups that operate within this context is determined by income and occupation and education; consequently it covers what people would normally understand by 'social class' and 'status'. Much has been said already about the linguistic implications of the diversity of roles that arise within those socio-economic contexts, but there is a further consequence of this diversity which relates to the 'social history' of the individuals who have to live with it. In our society the entry condition for many jobs is broadly educational, so that success at school has become a most important agent of social mobility. In consequence, a large number of people now lead lives as adults very different from those which they led as children. From a linguistic point of view, this means that they have had to cope with a very large number of wholly new situations for which initially the relevant ways of speaking were not available. Hence one of the most interesting linguistic questions in this area is how people learn the new speech habits that rapid social, occupational and educational change requires of them.

The third category, the POWER system, provides the social contexts for the exercise of control over others. Our deepest intuitions about the nature of 'society' are reflected in our concern for the role of authority in giving cohesion to the groups of which it is composed. In fact, the idea of 'social control' is central to the idea of 'society' itself.

> "Social control . . . refers to the various means used by a society to bring its recalcitrant members back into line. No society can exist without social control. Even a small group of people meeting but occasionally will have to develop their mechanisms of control if the group is not to dissolve in a very short time."
>
> (Berger)

From a linguistic point of view, the most interesting question is how language is drawn upon to provide those 'mechanisms of control', what part it then plays in the internal organisation of the social group concerned, and how a newcomer acquires command of the

98

requisite 'meanings'. Alternatively, one can ask how a man indicates his assumption of authority over others and what responses they are required to make. Even 'A-ten-shun' is a linguistic act to which a given response has to be *learnt*. The relevance of this to the social context of the school scarcely needs mention. What must be said, however, is that the linguistic means used for exercising social control tend to be very much tied to one particular context. This will be well known to people who have worked in several different schools or offices or factories.

Whatever the social context, however, an important aspect of social control is the existence of a hierarchy, or chain of command, and the relevant 'mechanisms of control' which operate through it are very often linguistic. Consider a common order of seniority that runs from headmaster, through deputy-head, senior staff, junior staff, senior pupils to junior pupils, and compare how each group in this order would (a) address other members of the group; (b) address a member of a group immediately above or below it; (c) address someone at a distance from it, like a first-former to Head of English, third-former to headmaster. Much more than the actual title of address, 'Sir' or 'Headmaster' or 'Brown', is involved. 'Address' really means a whole way of speaking through which one individual indicates to another his understanding of their mutual status and relationship. Consider, also, the differences between 'John', 'John Brown', 'Brown', 'You!', 'Come here!'. This sequence reveals another aspect of using language for social control, the part it plays in what the sociologist calls 'social distance', for 'John' represents a very narrow gap between speaker and spoken to, whereas the gap revealed by 'Come here' is very wide. The metaphor suggests that 'closeness' goes with intimacy and a personal response, whereas 'distance' goes with a denial of intimacy and an impersonal response. Parents and teachers intuitively modify the social distance between themselves and children or pupils in order to exercise control over them. The child knows the difference in the forcefulness and the urgency of the control being exercised between "Johnnie, run along now and have your bath", and "Get into that bath this minute!" Just as the pupil knows the difference between "Come and help me with the nets, will you?" and "You! Come here!" Moreover, they know what these differences are because they have learnt the meaning of the phrases in the particular social context of that home and that school.

The last of the four categories, VALUE INTEGRATION, is closely related to the third, because we are accustomed to justifying or defending much of our exercise of social control, and this involves us in the use of a language of value and judgement. If the first category is concerned with 'who comes from where', then the fourth involves 'right or wrong', the individual's view of moral reality. One bridge between the third and the fourth categories is provided by those linguistic 'mechanisms of control' which Berger lists as ". . . . Persuasion, ridicule, gossip and opprobrium". He goes on to say that,

> ". . . . in group discussions going on over a period of time individuals modify their originally held opinions to conform to the group norm, which corresponds to a kind of arithmetic mean of all the opinions represented in the group".

This quotation describes the process of integrating values operating at the level of the intimate social group, but the same principle can be seen at work throughout a society. The idea of 'political consensus' is an expression of just such an 'arithmetic mean'. Much of what is commonly understood by 'class' is equally the expression of, and response to, sets of values that are performing an experientially cohesive function for particular social groups within a society.

The characteristically middle class emphasis upon 'accent' and 'usage' expresses a complex relationship between 'getting and spending', which entitles you to a certain status; 'mechanisms of control', by means of which you mobilise that status to exercise control over others; and 'right and wrong', the need to justify exercising such control when it derives from a status based upon 'getting and spending'. The crucial part played by language in this process has provided subject matter for comedy both high and low since the 16th Century, and one of the most thorough intuitive explorations of it is to be found in the novels of Jane Austen. Again and again, her characters display, in their actions, the intimate connection between status and the linguistic expression of values as a means of exercising social control. Elinor in *Sense and Sensibility*, D'Arcy in *Pride and Prejudice* are particularly clear examples.

This connection between status, social control, and the expression of values is at the very centre of a school's existence. In the sense that

100

a school functions as a social group within a discernible social context, it is a speech community: there will be patterns of inter-action peculiar to the school, and consequently, there will also be patterns of language in use peculiar to it, and those who work together in the school develop common responses to them. Some-thing has been said already about the way in which the teachers in a school come to share a common view of the linguistic behaviour appropriate to learning, or to the roles of teacher and pupil. These are examples of the way in which a school creates a climate of opinion, or operates a system of value-integration, because it func-tions as a 'speech community'. It is for reasons such as this, therefore, that Labov put forward the idea that a speech community was best seen as

".. . a social group which shares *the same set of values* in regard to language rather than the group which uses language *in the same way.*"

In other words, there is little point in teachers arguing about pupils' use of written English, unless they are willing to make explicit the values which lead them to judge a certain way of writing as good or bad for the job.

5

The final section of this chapter is concerned with the mechanisms by which the newcomer enters into the life of a group. The new-comer may be the new-born child of the group, the family into which he is born. The newcomer may be the growing child as he comes into contact with an ever-widening circle of social groups: the newcomer may be the pupil new to the class, the student new to his college, the teacher new to a school. In every case where an individual enters a new social context, a process of social learning must take place, for he has to discover how to meet the demands of the interaction to which this new context gives rise. This is the process by means of which an individual finds out who he is, what rights he has, and what obligations he must undertake in relation to a particular social context:

"What happens in socialisation is that the social world is internal-ised within the child. The same process, though perhaps weaker

101

in quality, occurs every time the adult is initiated into a new social group".

(Berger)

From the point of view of the linguistic exploration of society, it is the most important of all social processes, because it is the process by which the individual is related to society through the medium of language. A newcomer learns about the social world he has entered through interacting with the other people in it, but interaction necessarily involves the use of language, so that knowledge of this world will come to him primarily through the medium of language. The 'meanings' that others reveal through their use of language are the 'meanings' that he must acquire in order to be able to share their social world.

The process of primary socialisation, the individual's initiation into a social world through the agency of his family, fundamentally shapes his understanding of the possibilities for social action that are open to him and determine his interpretation of the actions of others; consequently, it decisively influences his own actions and his judgements of others. It provides him with his initial knowledge of the culture of his community, and culture is:

". . . that complex whole which includes knowledge, belief, art, morals, law, custom and any other capabilities and habits acquired by man as a member of society".

(Tylor)

'The habits of the tribe' are then the actual expression of these capabilities in the everyday actions of ordinary people in a particular society. The important thing about these habits is that they are taken for granted because they are learnt in the course of growing up in, and becoming a member of, a society. They are learnt, however, through interaction with others, the members of child's family, his neighbours, the local community, and so on, and thus an essential aspect of learning these habits is learning the linguistic behaviour through which they are expressed. Another quotation in Chapter Two suggested that language was

". . . a complex inventory of all the ideas, interests and occupations that take up the attention of the community."

(Sapir)

That is to say, in the terms of this argument, language is itself not only one of the 'habits of the tribe' but also the chief vehicle for the transmission of those habits from one generation to the next. Language plays a vital part in the acquisition of culture, its maintenance, and its shaping effect upon social action, because knowledge of 'the habits of the tribe' and the linguistic competence necessary for expressing that knowledge are acquired at one and the same time. As the process of social learning involved in socialisation is highly specific, however, the way in which an individual learns to language these habits will depend upon who he is, where he lives, and what he does. Even more importantly, it will determine the way in which he interprets how others language their own understanding of them.

From a linguistic point of view, the most relevant work in this area has been done by Professor Bernstein. It has already made its appearance in Chapter 3 and it is central to the discussion of the role of language in the process of socialisation. It has also become quite widely known amongst teachers during the course of the last ten years, though it has not always been well understood. There is no room within the scope of this book to give it the detailed attention that it deserves, but the interested reader will find a good account of it in Denis Lawton's book, *Social Class, Language and Education*, Chapter V, and its implications for teaching and learning will be taken up by the present author in *Language: social means and social ends*.

Professor Bernstein asked the question, "How does the child learn what is relevant to the workings of social structure?" and answered it by pointing to the fact that social structure is realised through patterns of interaction, and patterns of interaction involve specific patterns of language in use: consequently, social structure determines the child's capacity to language. Language carries 'the habits of the tribe', but the child's language is shaped by the social context in which he learns it; therefore, his knowledge of these habits will be determined by the social context within which he grows up.

"As a child learns his speech, . . . he learns the requirements of his social structure."

A fundamental constraint upon being able to use language to live, or to use it as "... a link in concerted human activity ..." is, therefor, the fact that:

"Between language and speech there is social structure".

The social structure within which a child grows up creates a mesh between his knowledge *of* the language and his ability to use it on any particular occasion, because 'language' is the equivalent of 'meaning potential' and 'speech' the equivalent of 'language in use'. In particular, it should be remembered that a man's 'models of language' are acquired in the process of learning how to 'mean'; they do not form part of his 'meaning potential'. Therefore, a child's intuitive understanding of what language can be used for is open to the shaping force of the social structure within which he learns 'how to mean'.

The quotation in the Foreword of this book has it that:

"Language intervenes between man and nature acting upon him internally and externally."

The relationship between language and social structure that Professor Bernstein proposes would suggest a complementary version of this quotation that might read:

"Society intervenes between man and language acting upon him internally and externally."

This aspect of his work is expressed most clearly in the idea of the linguistic code, known to most people by the labels *restricted* and *elaborated*. The effect of social structure acting through the process of socialisation, the agency of the family and the medium of language, is to determine the basis of a speaker's view of both linguistic and social reality. A code is a term for the relationship between a pattern of social structure and a pattern of *language in use*. It is an abstraction at the level of 'grammar' or 'language' itself, and it refers to a speaker's view of how he can language: it does *not* refer to 'meaning potential'. In the terms of the next chapter, a code enters into the process by which the speaker interprets a situation and then makes a plan to guide his selection of the 'elements and structure' that he needs. (See p. 33). Therefore, the terms *elaborated* and *restricted*

104

refer to characteristic ways of using language to interact with other human beings: they do not suggest that there are two kinds of 'meaning potential'.

The importance of this for the teacher cannot be overstated, because it shows that a pupil's use of language is a result of the way in which he has learnt to use language in his own social world. The teacher who says, "They don't have language" misses the point entirely, because he is focused upon what he regards as a lack of 'meaning potential'. His pupils possess the 'meaning potential', but what they have not had experience of is a social world which yields the patterns of language in use that the teacher expects. The implications of this for the class-room are the subject of the next chapter.

FURTHER READING

P. L. Berger, *Invitation to Sociology* (Penguin).

B. Bernstein, "Social Class, Language and Socialization" in *Class, Codes and Control*, Vol. I (Routledge).

P. S. Doughty, *Language: social means and social ends* (Edward Arnold, forthcoming).

J. R. Firth, *The Tongues of Men* (O.U.P.).

R. Frankenberg, *Communities in Britain* (Penguin).

E. Hall, *The Silent Language* (Doubleday).

M. A. K. Halliday, *Grammar, Society and the Noun* (An Inaugural Lecture, published for University College, London, by H. K. Lewis and Co, [London]).

M. A. K. Halliday, "Language in a Social Perspective" in *The Context of Language*, Education Review, Vol. 23, No. 3, 1971).

M. A. K. Halliday, "The Functional Basis of Language", in (ed.) B. Bernstein, *Class, Codes and Control*, Vol. II (Routledge) and Halliday, *Explorations in the Functions of Language* (Edward Arnold).

D. Lawton, "A Critique of Bernstein's work on language and social class", Chapter 5 of *Social Class, Language and Education* (Routledge).

J. B. Pride, "Sociolinguistics" in *New Horizons in Linguistics* (ed. J. Lyons, Penguin).

W. J. H. Sprott, "Society: what is it and how does it change?" in *Basic Readings in the Sociology of Education* (ed. D. F. Swift [Routledge]).

Seven   Command of a language

1

Through the last four chapters a picture has been built up of man the language user. The discussion focused upon the degree to which language enters into every aspect of our lives as ordinary individuals and members of society. Insofar as it was relevant to the problems of teaching and learning, it was because those activities make use of language as much as, if not more than, any other human activity. In this chapter, the discussion has to move towards a much more direct involvement with the class-room. It is concerned with the way in which a speaker extends his command over spoken and written language, and begins by considering how this occurs as a normal and necessary part of using language to live. It continues by looking at the implications of this normal process for the particular context of school and college. The underlying argument is that there needs to be a careful consideration of the relationship between the processes every human being uses to extend his command of his language in the normal course of his daily life, and the deliberate attempts that teachers make in the class-room to achieve the same end. Unlike the rest of the book, therefore, this chapter ends by making particular recommendations about what might happen in the classroom, but only because these recommendations can be shown to follow from the general argument about competence set out at the beginning.

Competence is the individual's ability to use his own language. Its foundations are laid during that initial period between ten months and three years in the course of which the very young child acquires the basic 'elements and structure' of his mother tongue. From a linguistic point of view, this is a period of enormously rapid and comprehensive activity, which is followed by a more extended but no less remarkable period, from approximately age three to age seven, during which the child fills out and consolidates the knowledge *of* his language that the initial period has provided. It is necessary to distinguish between this process of language acquisition as it occurs in the young child and the 'command of language' that is the subject of this chapter, because the early stages of language acquisition possesses unique features. The young child uses mental processes that are unconscious and genetically programmed to deal with the enormous complexity of natural language. Put a child in a normal social environment where it will be in continuous contact with other speakers of a language and it will acquire that language, unless there is a pathological condition present to prevent it. This innate facility for acquiring language, however, relates to initial acquisition; although it remains an essential part of any later acquisition, after the earliest years the process is not in the same sense involuntary. All the same, some of the processes the child develops at that time continue to play an essential part in the later growth of competence, because they involve the way in which the brain is designed to language. In particular, the part played by interaction always retains its importance as a basic element in extending command of a language, because it requires the user to relate the patterns of the language directly to the purposes for which it is being used and the social context in which its use occurs.

One aspect of the basic distinction between acquiring language and extending competence applies as much to written as to spoken language. Although the teaching of writing occurs long after the initial maturational phase of language acquisition, a child is still faced at some stage with the task of acquiring the patterns of the writing system. Once this initial period of acquisition has led to a successful basic command of the system, he will then stand in relation to it as he stands in relation to the patterns of the language iself. Once a child has achieved initial command of the patterns of both spoken and written language, it is then possible to talk about the growth of competence as a process which embraces both modes. The actual acquisition of a writing-system, however, is a very different matter from the acquisition of a natural language insofar as it is dependent upon a deliberate process of instruction, usually in a formal learning situation. The initial teaching of reading and writing is a very large topic that lies outside the scope of this book, but reference is made in the Further Reading at the end of Chapter 9 to a number of relevant titles. What will concern the argument is the way in which growth of competence in writing can be encouraged or inhibited by particular procedures in the class-room. In particular, a theory of competence must say something about the inter-relationship of speaking and writing and the links between growth of competence in the one and in the other.

Before going on to look at the question of competence, however, it will be useful to sum up what has been said so far in this book about

107

language, because the nature and processes of competence must be seen to follow from the nature and function of language. The reader also needs to be able to see the direct links between language, competence and any subsequent recommendations extending command of a language in the class-room. From this point of view, there are four relevant propositions about language and together they make explicit the theory of language that underlies this book. "A theory of language" is a rational and explicit attempt to answer questions which ask why language is as it is, rather than what one particular language contains or how its parts fit together. These four propositions are one way of formulating certain basic principles about the nature and function of language, but, however they are formulated, their substance must appear in any theory of language that is relevant to the linguistic problems of teaching and learning. Such a theory must be able to offer a rational and explicit account of competence and only a theory that incorporated the substance of these four propositions would be in a position to do so. Stated in bald outline, they are:

(1) that language enables the user to construct an unlimited number of utterances out of a limited number of individual 'elements and structures',
(2) that the capacity to language has a biological basis,
(3) that languaging is behaving,
(4) that the act of languaging is a process of making meanings.

2

The first proposition is the most difficult to grasp, because it involves a way of thinking about the internal structure and organisation of language that has little to represent it in a speaker's common understanding of linguistic reality. At the centre of the difficulty is the fact that 'words' are habitually regarded as the equivalent of language. For T. S. Eliot, in the "Four Quartets", writing is

> ". . . the intolerable wrestle
> With words and meanings . . .",

and later, it is "Trying to learn to use words . . .". In saying this, he is representing at his own creative level the folk-linguistic intuition that 'words' are what language is about. To most people, the really difficult part of using language seems to be a matter of choosing the

108

right 'word' for the occasion, for they are sure that there would never be a problem "if only they could find the words for it". It is rather like the response to cartoon films. The audience knows that the animator's hand determines all the movements, but they actually respond to Tom and Jerry as though they are characters free to come and go like actors. Tom and Jerry are the 'words' of the action that the audience is focused upon and the 'structure' provided by the animator's pen does not really enter their thoughts as they watch. When teachers focus upon command of language for learning, the suggestion is usually that what pupils need is more 'vocabulary', whereas the pupils' problem is much more likely to be a matter of the 'elements and structure' involved. A pupil may well have all the individual items of vocabulary that he needs and still give the impression that he lacks the command of language for learning which the situation requires. What he needs to be saying to himself is not "Why can't I find the words for it?", but "If only I could put together the words I have in such a way that their organisation would then convey the meanings which I intend."

Any particular act of languaging, like this sentence, or asking the way, or lecturing on the Industrial Revolution, is the end product of a process of selection. A language can be seen as a very large collection of individual items, of many different types, and any actual utterance, written or spoken, as a particular selection of them put together so as to form a single coherent whole. A useful working analogy is provided by construction sets like Meccano. They provide the model-maker with a whole range of parts, strips, plates, wheels, rods, cogs and so on. Each type of part has a particular function to perform in the building system, strips to provide the framework, plates to give covering, rods and pulleys and cogs to give movement, but each type is only made available in a certain number of set lengths, widths or diameters, so that there may be strips, 2, 4 or 6 inches long, but not $7\frac{1}{4}$, $13\frac{2}{3}$ or $21\frac{2}{9}$ inches. In similar fashion, a language provides its speakers with a small number of basic components, types of 'elements' like noun and verb, types of 'structure' like phrase and clause, and other features that are less easily spoken of in common language terms like tense and mood and case. All these basic types of component contain a number of different 'lengths' and 'widths'. This was recognised in the traditional grammatical terminology that most readers are likely to have met, where nouns could be 'concrete' or 'abstract', clauses could be

109

'adjectival', or 'adverbial', tenses 'past', 'present' or 'future', and so on. Whatever the description used, or the terms employed, the basic assumption is the same. The number of possible types of noun, or clause, or tense is limited, and each type is clearly distinguishable from the other. A selection of both 'elements and structure', chosen from all the components available to the speaker, goes to the fashioning of every actual utterance, and the selection will depend upon the speaker's assessment of the needs of the moment.

From this point of view, the essential thing about a language is that it is composed of a large store of many different types of 'elements and structure', invariable in their nature and function, which can be put together, however, by the act of languaging to meet the needs of innumerable specific situations. The next step is to see what other principles follow from this view of the internal organisation of a natural language. The two most important involve the idea of rules and the question of choice. It is possible to make working models out of Meccano, as long as the parts are assembled according to a small number of basic rules that govern the ways in which they can be put together. Bolts have to have nuts, pulleys must run free, cogs must engage, structures must be rigid, and so on. Similarly, language functions as long as a speaker puts together 'elements and structure' according to the linguistic rules that govern the possibilities for their combination in his language. To take a handful of obvious examples from English English: there has to be concord in number and person between subject and verb; the words in the phrase 'that very beautiful girl' must be used in that order and no other, whereas the words in 'old upright brown chairs' can be re-ordered in more than one way, the phrase still remains meaningful; the pattern of "Did he come back?" can only be used when a question is intended whereas "He did come back" can be a statement or a question according to the intonation with which it is said; similarly "He did come back" is a pattern meaning 'affirmative', whereas "He did not come back", is a pattern meaning 'negative'. As a major part of the process of languaging is conducted by activities of the brain that remain unconscious to the speaker, however, linguistic rules need to be understood as deep and abstract principles governing language function rather than a list of 'do's' and 'don'ts' that the user applies in the act of languaging if he has a mind to. When a linguist sets out to describe the grammar of a language, his aim is to discover what those linguistic rules are and which combinations of 'elements and

110

structure' are therefore possible and which are not. Therefore it is right to speak of a grammar as an expression of the rules which govern the patterns of linguistic function that constitute the structure of a language.

If a language is both a store of 'elements and structure' and a set of rules which govern their meaningful combination and use, then it follows that using language necessarily involves a process of selection determined by the way in which the rules apply to a particular situation. An actual utterance can only represent the combination of a small selection from the total store, so that the making of an utterance must involve choice. It is this aspect of choice in the process of languaging that holds the balance between the fixed or predetermined nature of the internal organisation of a language, the store of 'elements and structure', and the endlessly varying demands of the actual situation in which its speakers are called upon to use it. Returning for a moment to the analogy of the construction set, the enormous delight of Meccano is that it provides endless scope for free invention. Once the model maker knows what parts he has and how they go together, he can devise a very large number of individual models of many different shapes, sizes, and purposes. He is limited by four things only, the number of parts he has, the way they are designed to be put together, his grasp of the rules governing their combination, and his own inventiveness.

The same four basic constraints will still apply, however, if he is devising utterances instead of models. In particular, the last of the four, inventiveness, plays a crucial part in his command of a language. 'Inventiveness' does not, however, necessarily mean 'originality' or 'creativity' in the common sense of the words. It is built up from at least six different factors in his experience. Set out as they apply to his activities as a model maker, they can be distinguished as:

(1) his over-all familiarity with the system of construction involved
(2) the opportunities he has had to test out its possibilities by making actual models
(3) his freedom to choose what models he wants to make
(4) his freedom to find out what cannot be done by being allowed to make his own mistakes
(5) tolerance from adults when they see his efforts apparently

111

departing from their recollection of the models in the Pattern
Book

(6) his knowledge of what kinds of things there are to make.

'Inventiveness' is thus the ability to draw upon a wide experience of
the constructional system in question to meet the needs of a particular problem, in this case the model the boy wants to build. In the
context of using language, therefore, 'inventiveness' is the equivalent
of competence, the ability to draw upon a wide experience of
the language system in order to meet the linguistic needs of a particular occasion for using language.

3

The second of these four propositions about language asserts that
language has a biological basis, an idea which has already been
explored in Chapters 3 and 4. The activity of languaging is not a
by-product of man's greatly enlarged cerebral capacity, or the outcome merely of a generalised 'intelligence' that follows from it, but
the consequence of processes that are inherent in the species and
specific to it. In this sense learning and using language is as much a
'natural' part of being human as walking upright or seeing in colour.
As human beings, we are provided with a capacity for learning
language, but this capacity represents no more than an innate potential. That potential is realised through the acquisition of a mother
tongue and that process requires continuous interaction with competent speakers of the language. Learning one's own language is,
therefore, the outcome of using a general capacity that is genetically
programmed, in a multiplicity of particular social contexts.

This second proposition has two important implications for the question of competence. An individual human being is designed to
language, and the process of languaging has built into it the capacity
to learn language. Consequently, growth of competence will be most
successfully achieved when this capacity is deliberately exploited for
the purpose. In addition, learning one's own language is a question
of learning what utterances are appropriate to what social contexts.
An individual speaker will always be presented with new situations
and find himself in the position of having to learn what utterances
are appropriate to those situations. The process of learning a language, therefore, can never really be said to be complete because

there always remains the possibility of a situation occurring that will lie outside an individuals' previous experience.

The third proposition about language is already very familiar to readers of this book, because the idea that language is a species of human behaviour underlies the whole notion of exploring language. As it comes in this sequence of propositions, it follows logically from the idea of languaging as a capacity with its basis in the biological make-up of the species. An individual's knowledge of his language, and his command of it, are broadly determined by his cumulative experience as a member of innumerable human groups, from the family to the nation, and embracing all aspects of his life. In this sense, to language *is* to behave, and no piece of folk wisdom is more confusing than the demand for "Actions, not words." Human behaviour always exists in the context of a particular culture, but a culture modifies and shapes behaviour primarily through the medium of language. Language in use is, therefore, a species of social and cultural behaviour.

For these reasons, and looked at from the point of view of the teacher, language is necessarily the least independent of all the areas of learning with which he is likely to have to concern himself. It is the least independent, because there is no point at which it is meaningful to separate language as social and cultural behaviour in the world at large from language for learning in the class-room, because language for learning is but one example of language as social and cultural behaviour. Growth of competence is a necessary feature of language in use, and language in use is a necessary part of normal social and cultural behaviour. Extending a pupil's command over language for learning is therefore only a particular instance of growth of competence in the context of a formal learning situation. Unless he were deliberately required to do so, a pupil would not normally leave his accumulated experience of language learning outside when he entered the class-room. To consider 'English Language' as a school subject, circumscribed by the tight boundaries of syllabus, examination, and departmental responsibilities, and thus rendered recognisably distinct from all other use of English as a natural language, is to mistake the problem entirely. It can lead only to the ultimate absurdity of the following quotation from a Chief Examiner's report on O-Level English Language:

"Since so many candidates take English Language at O-Level

without having any special aptitude for the subject, it is not surprising that many essays are pedestrian and unambitious."

Competence is not a matter of having a 'special aptitude for the subject', but a normal and necessary aspect of human behaviour, the use of language to live. Unless a theory of competence takes this into account, it is unlikely to have much to contribute to a discussion of language for learning.

The last of the four propositions follows logically from the third in the same way that the third followed the second. Once it is said that language is a form of human behaviour, its existence must be explainable in terms of its value for the species, and this value lies in its enormous potential for recording, sorting, categorising, and ordering experience and then making it possible to share the results of this process with other speakers of a language. It is for this reason that

". . . the grammatical system of a language is closely related to the social and personal needs that language is required to serve." (M. A. K. Halliday)

Therefore, it can be said to provide its speakers with a 'meaning potential'. The activity of languaging is then a process of realising this 'meaning potential' in particular social and cultural contexts.

A speaker expects his 'meaning' to be understood, and to be able to make meaning out of what is said to him: the old phrase, "Do you take my meaning?" expressed a powerful insight into the workings of language. This assumption, however, takes for granted the fact that language must be ordered and predictable in its organisation in order that 'meanings' can be both given and taken. The irritation that many readers have felt with twentieth-century writers like Dylan Thomas or James Joyce has its origin in their disregard for the ways in which the 'meaning potential' of English is realised through a particular and predictable pattern of speaking and writing.

A speaker is also inclined to take it for granted that his particular social and cultural experience has been shared by those he is talking to, so that he is disturbed when they fail to take his 'meanings' and seldom questions the degree to which he himself has failed to 'mean', because his own use of 'elements and structure' has been governed by experience that they have not shared. Unless a speaker is aware of this possibility, his attempts to language in an unfamiliar situation,

114

or one in which the other participants do not share his experience of languaging, is likely to prove sadly ineffective. This is most relevant to the class-room, for the large majority of teachers have had a cumulative experience of using language that is very different from that of their pupils and even their students.

4

In the previous three sections of this chapter, a theory of language has been set out so as to provide the point of departure for exploring competence. The most important factor in exercising command of a language is the degree to which use of language depends upon the speakers' intuitive assessment of the situation in which he has to use it, whether in speech or in writing. He would not use the same way of speaking or writing in communicating to the press, negotiating a contract, outlining a project to a fellow specialist, or confessing his domestic difficulties to a close friend. The process of matching language to particular social contexts is something that teachers are likely to take for granted: consequently they tend to overlook the linguistic complexity of the operations involved. What makes it possible for them to language with such facility themselves is their own cumulative experience of using language; as adult native speakers of English, their acquaintance with a very wide range of ways of speaking and writing English has been long and continuous. The delicate process of matching a particular pattern of language to a particular context has become so much a part of their total experience of using language that they easily forget how prolonged a period of learning was involved before they reached this degree of fluency.

From the point of view of competence, the determining feature in any social context is the audience for what is said or written: the other people present in the situation or the intended readers. It is the user's intuitive assessment of his audience that leads to his choice of a particular way of speaking or writing. The response of the audience then provides him with a check upon the accuracy of his initial interpretation of the needs of the situation. Obviously, the major difference between speaking and writing is the immediacy of the response. Face-to-face situations require the speaker to adjust his discourse continuously in response to the reactions or replies of the others present. The ability to choose a way of writing or speaking appropriate to a given situation does indeed depend upon the

115

accurate interpretation of the audience involved and this, in turn, depends upon an individual's cumulative experience of audiences and situations. Thus an essential factor in the growth of competence is the individual's readiness to experience unfamiliar situations and his ability to generalise that experience for use in analogous situations in the future. Obviously, he cannot experience them if they are not available to him, nor can he show readiness if his experience of new situations has been very limited. If he lacks readiness, his tentativeness in new situations will seriously inhibit his ability to generalise from them.

Assessing the audience, therefore, necessarily involves a process of interpretation, but both situations and ways of speaking and writing are very variable in the demands that they make upon the speaker's ability to interpret. While the social chat of a family at breakfast requires minimal assessment from all concerned, because the same situation occurs every day and all those present know each other intimately, something like an open-ended discussion at sixth form or college level makes enormous demands upon the interpretative ability of those taking part. In this case, the needs of the situation change continuously as the discussion proceeds and anyone involved in it is required to reinterpret the situation each time he speaks. (See Chapter 8, p. 129.)

The work of school or college makes progressively greater demands upon a pupil's powers of interpretation as he moves on from year to year. The teachers concerned are often unaware of the demands that they are making, because of their own familiarity with the subject, and they do not see that the ways of writing and speaking which they regard as most appropriate can, in themselves, constitute a formidable challenge to the existing competence of those in their classes.

The idea of interpretation can be explored further by looking more closely at three aspects of language use; the user's knowledge *of* a language; his knowledge of situations; and the process by which he determines what to say or write in any particular situation. The first of these has been discussed already in Chapter 2. To recapitulate, knowledge of a language embraces both the individual's potential for speaking or writing, his linguistic resource, and his ability to draw upon it in putting together particular utterances. A speaker, however, is only in a position to language after he has worked out the features of the social context for which the languaging is intended. Interpretation is therefore essential to the activity of languaging which means that an individual's cumulative knowledge of situations must be regarded as an essential part of his 'knowledge of language'.

The speaker, therefore, looks two ways in the process of languaging: outwards, for an interpretation of the situation and its audience— inwards, to make the necessary selection from his linguistic resource. Competence is thus a process that mediates between social context and 'meaning potential'. Metaphorically speaking, a speaker makes an assessment of a situation, draws up a plan for the language that it demands and then selects the necessary 'elements and structure' from his linguistic resource to match the specifications of the plan. This selection is not made once and for all, however, for one particular situation. A speaker makes his initial assessment, but the plan that results from this will have to be modified continuously in the light of all that is said and done in the course of the subsequent interaction.

The speaker who loses touch with his audience is only too familiar a figure. According to this analysis, he is someone who works out a plan for the situation as it is initially, but then continues to use his original plan rather than revise it in response to the reactions of his audience. In writing, however, the process is more complex. As a writer rereads a draft, he will be trying to match what he has written against his idea of the needs and expectations of his audience. The key factor that he has to assess, before drawing up his plan, is his idea of his audience, because it defines the particularity of the situation to which his 'meanings' are directed. Any modification to the draft will, therefore, come from an assessment of the match between the language of the particular draft in question and the writer's over-all interpretation of his audience's needs and expectations.

A speaker's competence, then, mediates between his potential for making meanings, and situations in which he is called upon to speak and write; it is the sum total of his ability to interpret a social context, work out a plan for it, and use that plan to select 'elements and structure' that will language what he wants to 'mean' in that context. Most current attempts to meet the linguistic needs of the pupils

117

and students, however, make the assumption that a basic lack of 'meaning potential' or 'linguistic resource' is what prevents their producing acceptable written work. What evidence there is, however, suggests that a pupil's written work is often a very poor indication of his total 'meaning potential', especially if the bulk of what he is asked to write is in the form of notes and essays for particular subject specialists. If the alternative assumption is, therefore, made— that pupils do, in fact, possess the necessary *potential*, but have not had sufficient relevant experience of using language in the contexts concerned—then the teacher's task is to create situations in which the required growth of competence can take place. In this process, the relationship between language, social context, and growth of competence plays a decisive part.

It is necessary to provide a wide range of learning situations which will require many different ways of speaking and writing. Patterns of work are wanted which depend upon the collaboration of several members of a class, and the active participation of the teacher in the role of 'experienced adult user of language'. In this way, pupils will be able to learn that speaking and writing is the product of a continuous process of interpretation and planning, because the situation in which they are engaged as speakers or writers will be continuously changing. What such a situation looks like is discussed in detail in the following chapter and the units of *Language in Use* show how it can be brought about in the class-room. The essential point is that the social context of the class-room must make use of the way in which human beings are designed to develop command of a language. The need to do this, moreover, can now be seen to arise out of the nature of language itself and not out of theories about 'teaching method', the so-called 'whims of the progressives', the demands of the subject curriculum, the public examinations, or the pressures of public opinion.

5

The extension of a pupil's command of language for learning so that it will embrace several distinguishable varieties of the language, both spoken and written, is fundamental to the whole process of formal learning. Ideally, the pupil or student should be able to narrow the gap for himself between what he can initially bring to the class-room and what is habitually expected of him when he gets there. Many teachers now face pupils or students, however, for whom the gap is so great that it is unlikely to close. To meet this situation, they demand that English Departments return to traditional practices in teaching English language, those of direct instruction in spelling and punctuation and syntax. The evidence suggests, however, that these methods do not lead to growth of competence. For one thing, they do not take into account the fact that an apparent failure in the class-room may only involve a small area of a pupil's total capacity to language. If this 'failure' is then taken as a true measure of a pupil's competence, and even of his intelligence, the remedies advanced to meet this 'failure' are likely to be ineffective, because they will be focused upon one small area where competence is as yet underdeveloped, instead of the large areas in which it is already well-developed and therefore available as a springboard towards further development.

If a teacher's attention is restricted to what goes wrong, he is likely to overlook the fact that growth in a student's ability to use language for learning is dependent upon the range and quality of the language for learning that he experiences. For instance, there is a positive relationship between a pupil's cumulative experience of learning situations in which talk is asked for, and the growth of his facility in responding to the progressively steeper linguistic demands of the learning situations that progress through school and college present to him. If the range of situations which he experiences is restricted, he will not develop command of the ways of speaking used in formal learning, and, ultimately, that familiar gap will appear between his performance and his teachers' expectations. This is most commonly seen in the first years of secondary school, sixth form, and college.

There are two further aspects of competence which tend to get overlooked in many common-room discussions, the relationship between the use of spoken language and growth of competence in the use of written work, and the time-scale necessary for that growth to take place. Many teachers think about encouraging growth of competence only in relation to the writing of exposition and argument within the context of their own subject. The ability to handle other ways of writing does not concern them, nor do they associate the use of spoken language with the development of the written language that they look for, though they often comment upon their pupil's failure to enter into intelligent discussion. The theory of competence

119

put forward in this chapter, however, argues that an individual's competence, whether spoken or written, is the product of a single capacity: hence any growth in relation to one mode of using language is likely to have an effect upon the other, even though that effect may be indirect or delayed.

One feature of spoken language in formal learning situations will illustrate the point. The class are engaged in a course of study which requires a high level of both abstractness and generality. A point has been reached at which the class meet a concept that is central to the subject involved, a concept that can be summed up by a single term, however, like 'the Gentry', or 'imagery', or 'entropy', or 'marginal price'. The teacher uses the term itself in the course of his exposition and he is also likely to make use of the 'elements and structure' that characterise the variety of English normally employed in the systematic discussion of the field to which the concept belongs. In doing so, he will use a large number of words and phrases so familiar to him that he is likely to overlook their newness for his audience. Even if he is conscious of the problem posed by the variety in question, he has to give an explicit account of the concept involved and this necessarily requires him to use the public language appropriate to the task, a language which is *technical* in the proper sense of the word (see Glossary). The problem facing the class is as much linguistic as conceptual. They have both to understand the concept to which the term refers and learn how to use it meaningfully. Learning how to use a term is the equivalent of learning how to make a small extension in one's command of language for learning, but it involves knowledge of language, linguistic resource, competence, the experience of social contexts and the ability to interpret them. However small a task learning a new term may appear to be, it touches many aspects of languaging because 'learning' in this context means making a new combination out of an enormously complex interlocking store of 'elements and structure'. Thus it involves rather more than merely 'adding a word to their vocabulary'. A term of any real conceptual density like 'entropy' or 'symbiosis' or 'image' or 'fiction' will require modifications in many related areas of previously ordered experience, and the very least that can be said is that the process of learning to use it will require time and practice for its accomplishment.

Consider for a moment what happens when a term is used for the first time. Some of those in the class will find it familiar, some will only have heard of it, and for some it will be wholly new and unfamiliar. Everyone, however, will automatically try to match it to something already known from previous experience. If the term is 'Gentry', it will be matched with what is already known about the organisation of English society in the period under study, perhaps Tudor or Stuart, but ideas associated with the word 'gentleman' will also enter into the attempt to assimilate it. Obviously, the less familiar the field of study is to the class, or the more remote the term from anything in common usage, the less chance there is of its providing an adequate point of reference, and the more likely the class will be to grasp at any common associations the word may suggest, whether they are relevant or not. Notice, however, that in this particular case the class must be able to make use of the ideas of 'organisation' and 'society', both as terms in themselves and in relation to this particular period of English history, if they are to find a point of reference for the new term. A pupil or student who has only the vaguest idea of what a historian means by 'society' is unlikely to make much sense of 'Gentry', if the only gloss that his teacher provides is in terms of 'Society'. Consequently, every new term that is used in the course of an exposition necessarily relates to a large number of other terms, and while a teacher may be alert to the new term itself, he is much less likely to be aware of the difficulties raised by the other terms he uses, because he has ceased to think of them as terms at all. From a linguistic point of view, a term's range of reference, the number of other terms that are involved in understanding its significance, indicates the linguistic load that is placed upon the pupil when he is asked to use it; and the greater the load, the longer the time likely to be required for achieving that small growth of competence which effective use of the term will require.

Some teachers believe that the problem can be avoided by leaving out the use of terms altogether and relying upon common language for exposition. Being explicit in any field, however, requires the speaker or writer to make general statements and he can only do this by employing terms, because their job is to provide a means of making general statements with precision. Moreover, these statements are likely to be abstract, as well as general, because they will refer to objects and events, and will make rational propositions about their occurrence, at the same time. 'The Gentry' is not simply a collective noun for 'gentlemen of England' or 'men of substance'; it

121

advances a theory about the way in which a body of individuals conducted themselves in relation to the public affairs of their time. The difficulty for the student is not simply 'knowing the term', but, firstly, being able to grasp the propositions it makes about the sixteenth- and seventeenth-century English society, and then being able to find the appropriate linguistic means for discussing these propositions explicitly and rationally in both speech and writing.

Every reader of this book will be able to find a parallel for 'gentry' in his own experience. In the course of reading it, in fact, he may well have found himself in the same situation as his pupils or students. Entry into any field of human enquiry, even exploring language, lies through the language in which its representative thought structures are embodied. From a linguistic point of view, developing a familiarity with this language will involve a growth of competence, however small. Developing this familiarity, moreover, is as much a linguistic matter as a question of the ability to handle concepts, and serious misjudgements of the needs of particular pupils are likely to follow if these two are confused. A pupil's inability to achieve the desired growth of competence and his ability to handle the concepts involved may be related to each other. It is not wise to assume that he lacks the ability to handle concepts, until he has had the chance to develop the growth of competence which is a precondition for his being able to do so.

6

This section now presents an outline of growth of competence. It is set out in terms of actual class-room practice and is offered as a sketch map of what may be looked for in attempting to assess the course of the processes involved. For convenience in discussion, growth of competence can be divided into four stages, but it must be remembered that there are no hard and fast divisions between one stage and the next. The whole process is continuous within one individual. The four steps are recognition, familiarisation, hesitant command, and fluent command.

(1) Recognition
This is the initial stage of an individual's experience of new terms and new patterns. It is very often silent, and may seem passive. On the surface, it may look like an apparent unwill-

ingness to participate in discussion, or even apathetic withdrawal. The situation is typified by that first term in the secondary school or after O-Level, or at College, when a class is likely to find work disconcertingly heavy in its linguistic demands. So much that is new is going on that pupils and students can easily feel there is little they are able to contribute. Any aspect of their work is likely to present so much that is unfamiliar and in need of careful 'recognition' that they are made acutely aware of the present limits of their competence. They need to live with the newly recognised for some time before they can be expected to begin to be familiar with its use.

(2) Familiarisation

At this stage, individual items are likely to be used with hesitation; contributions are diffident, and there is a strong tendency to avoid discussion proper in favour of a conversational exploration of the topic; there may be a heavy reliance on personal anecdote apparently unrelated to the topic, and pupils and students are likely to want to use a way of speaking less formal than most teachers are readily willing to accept for the work in question. At this stage, consequently, there is great benefit to be gained from a pattern of working together which allows a great deal of interaction between members of the class, with the teacher available as consultant. Being occupied with the difficulty of contributing themselves, many individuals may be impatient of length in the contribution of others, and may be reluctant to listen to them; what is intended to be class discussion can thus become a set of disjointed monologues. Learning to tolerate delay is as much a social as a linguistic skill, but it is vital to the procedures of mature discussion, for this relies upon the convention that others present will allow a speaker time to develop his argument and make use of pauses for verbal planning. (See Chapter 8.) The variation between the length of time different individuals require at this stage is very great. This is the most difficult stage for the teacher to live with, but it is a stage that can be rushed only at the expense of inhibiting the long-term growth of competence in progress.

(3) Hesitant command

Here, hesitancy and tentativeness are marked, but the

participants begin to sound more adult in discussion; contributions are longer, there is some attempt to sustain objectivity, and the participants show that they are now more aware that other contributions must be tolerated and attended to. They also begin to show that they recognise one can participate fully simply by listening. The element of hesitancy is most apparent in the number of false starts, planning pauses, mismatches in selecting terms, awkwardness in handling strings of subordinate clauses, and uncertainty in the placing of comment forms, like 'conceivably', 'probably', 'certainly', and in grasping their inter-relationships. There is also awkwardness in handling the social aspects of engaging in an extended discussion, such as timing one's entry into it and responding to non-verbal information revealing each participant's attitude to progress of the discussion. It is at this stage that it is easy to confuse an uncertain control of the necessary linguistic forms with an inadequate grasp of the concept structure of the propositions being discussed. Both may be present, and each may contribute to the presence of the other, but it is vital to see that two elements ARE involved. The crucial problem for the teacher is establishing the exact relationship between them. If he focuses on one only, he is likely to make a judgement that will seriously underestimate the capacities of the pupil concerned, conceptual or linguistic.

(4) Fluent command

The talk now approximates to the pattern of adult discussion. The relevant terms are handled approximately and easily, and the individual contributions reveal a greater overall coherence. Pupils now realise that they can be active participants in the discussion without actually speaking. The most marked feature of this stage is the achievement of genuine responsiveness to the flow of the discussion, so that it is governed by the needs of the topic involved, rather than by the linguistic difficulties of the participants.

This outline refers to speech. The basic progression applies equally to growth of competence in writing, but three points should be noted. Firstly, *Recognition* will be closely linked with what pupils read; at this stage they need a wide acquaintance with texts that make use of the way of writing which they are trying to master. Secondly, the time-scale of this stage is likely to be very protracted, and the process of deriving support from what is being read continues during the later stages. Thirdly, proper familiarisation in writing is likely to take place outside the view of the teacher. It is contained in the first sketches, the crossings-out and rewritings, that should precede the production of a piece for his attention. What he needs to do is to see that there is time for this, and that his pupils understand its importance.

Given the conditions under which most written work is produced in school and college, most teachers never see anything more accomplished than *Hesitant command*, because the relationship between *Hesitant command* and *Fluent command* in writing is twofold. In one sense, *Fluent command* is the result of establishing a growth of competence. Once properly established, it is assumed to be available to the speaker or writer whenever he finds himself needing to language in a context to which it is appropriate. Everyone is familiar, however, with the way one can run through a contribution to a discussion before it is made, or rehearse a contribution to some particularly difficult situation that impends, like an interview or public lecture. Similarly, however fluent a man's command of a way of writing, he will seldom, if ever, achieve an entirely satisfactory version at a first attempt. It would seem that the kind of writing most often required of pupils, moreover, rational exposition and argument, is precisely the kind of writing that is most dependent upon a careful and often extended process of *Hesitant command* before a text can be produced which an experienced reader would accept as fluent. The corollary of this is that most teachers cannot, therefore, expect to see very often a text which is truly fluent, because the writer is seldom allowed the time required, or given the motivation, for raising a hesitant version to a fluent version. The experience of writing both this book and *Language in Use* is that it takes between five and seven drafts to reach a final version, and even then reading the proofs will still reveal better ways of saying many of the things in them.

7

These four stages in the growth of competence can be collectively referred to as 'Rehearsal' for there is no doubt that the idea of rehearsing what is said or written is central to the whole question of exercising command of a language. The question now arises as to the possible relationship between rehearsal in speech, and any subsequent handling of similar topics in writing. This area is very obscure, but the theory of competence outlined in this chapter would suggest that this relationship is close and positive. What is rehearsed thoroughly in discussion first does seem to be more manageable should be a written account of it become necessary.

This relationship between rehearsal in speech and writing leads to the suggestion that the following sequence in the class-room would go a long way towards promoting a successful growth of competence:

(1) exploratory discussion to initiate a topic;
(2) work tasks carried out in groups involving collaborative discussion and planning;
(3) the writing of some kind of report by the groups;
(4) evaluative discussion by the class of the reports;
(5) a final stage involving rewriting in the light of both the evaluative discussion and further group discussion of its implications for individual reports.

This pattern shows how the essential interconnectedness of speech and writing can help to develop growth of competence, and the individual Units of *Language in Use* show how this pattern can be applied to a wide range of different class-room situations.

There are two further points to make and they concern teachers' and students' 'knowledge *about* language'. As was said in Chapter Two, all speakers of a language possess folk-linguistic ideas about what it is to language, and how language is, and ought to be, used in their society, and teachers usually have a very strongly developed folk-linguistic. Very often the effect of this folk-linguistic is to impose upon a class, struggling to achieve satisfactory *Hesitant command*, standards of usage which should be applied only to *Fluent command*. Moreover, these standards often derive from the idea that all written English ought to conform to that one model, 'good plain prose', which ignores the vital part played by the context itself in determining the way of speaking or writing most appropriate to it.

The moral of this is both simple and difficult. A teacher needs to understand his own folk-linguistic, and that of his pupils; and he ought to be ready to restrain his anxiety when faced with written

English which does not match his idea of what would be appropriate in the circumstances. If he is too ready to impose upon his class a model which they cannot yet handle, the result is likely to be a progressive deterioration in their written output, coupled with an increasing reluctance to produce written English at all. In this lies the difficulty, because the hardest thing to do in the class-room is to do nothing, and wait, when presented with what appears to be an immediate failure in a vital aspect of learning. Pupil's folk-linguistic very often includes the idea that competence is not open to any deliberate and conscious development. One way to tackle this problem is by starting with what pupils think they know about their language, and then drawing them into a consideration of what is really involved in the things they most take for granted. Again, this is a procedure that is frequently made use of in *Language in Use* and a quick glance at Units like A2 and G3 will show what such an enquiry would look like. Exploring language in this way can lead to a much readier acceptance of *Familiarisation* and *Hesitant command*, because it reveals that these activities are not merely a feature of learning how to use language in school or college, but an integral part of the way language is learnt in any human situation. Understanding how language relates him to the world and to others, moreover, can give a pupil the confidence to tackle language tasks which otherwise he would believe quite beyond him, because the process of exploring language in use lets him see that his own potential for language is greater than he thought and that his competence is not fixed once and for all by divine decree.

SUMMARY

Finally, here is a list of class-room procedures that have a direct effect upon growth of competence in any situation that calls for the use of language for learning;

(1) Giving full weight to continuous omnivorous reading. This requires supervision. Too often, teachers, assume that pupils and students can find appropriate books and periodicals without any help.

(2) Giving particular attention to exploratory talk in the class-room as this is a very important feature of *Familiarisation* and *Hesitant command*.

(3) Linking the exploratory talk to writing tasks which have a clearly defined goal that relates to the on-going work of the

class and is not merely devised in order to produce a piece of writing for marking.

(4) Developing a tolerance in pupils for *Familiarisation* and *Hesitant command* in both spoken and written language.

(5) Developing a tolerance for delay in the appearance of competence in relation to any particular kind of talking or writing.

(6) Abandoning the attempt to increase competence through the explicit presentation of knowledge about the language as this is represented in English language course books.

(7) Restraining the habit of close and continuous detailed correction of writing and speaking, so that much can go on which is open to revision and expansion by the pupils themselves.

(8) Providing an adequate specification for any use of language which is asked for, spoken or written. Without the specifications, pupils are being asked to language in a vacuum, because there is no 'situation' for them to interpret.

FURTHER READING

D. Barnes, "Language in the Secondary Class-room", in *Language, the learner and the school* (Penguin).

P. S. Doughty, *English in the curriculum*, in Papers in Linguistics and English Teaching, Series II (Longman).

P. S. Doughty, *Current Attitudes to Written English*, Nuffield Papers in Linguistics and English Teaching (Longman).

P. S. Doughty and G. M. Thornton, *Notes towards a theory of competence*, in Papers in Linguistics and English Teaching, Series II (Longman).

M. A. K. Halliday, *Language and Social Man*, in Papers in Linguistics and English Teaching, Series II (Longman).

M. A. K. Halliday, "Language structure and language function", *New Horizons in Linguistics*, ed. J. Lyons (Penguin).

C. Hannam, P. Smyth and N. Stephenson, *Young teachers and reluctant learners*, Chapters 6 and 7 (Penguin).

A. Talland, "Acquisitions of habits, skills and information", Chapter 2 of *Disorders of memory and learning* (Penguin).

Eight   Speech and talk

1

If somebody in a discussion group is asked the question, "What do you think, John?", he must decide in a second or so what to say and how to say it. Or rather, he must decide how to begin to say what he wants to say. He must draw upon the language stored in his brain to begin to build up the reply that he judges appropriate to the situation.

Since he is answering a question, he will begin with a grammatical structure, or the first part of a grammatical structure, appropriate to an answer, for example, "I agree . . ." He may then want to give reasons for his agreement, and will continue, "because . . ." and then go on to elaborate one or more reasons.

But a man in a discussion group is not producing his reasons in some kind of vacuum. He will be constantly aware of the other members of the group. Indeed, his position in the group, his relationship to the other members of it, his knowledge of the subject under discussion—factors like these will contribute not only to the way in which he begins to respond to the question, but will determine the way in which he shapes, and constantly reshapes, his answer. Afraid, possibly, that someone will interrupt him even before he begins his answer proper, he may, in fact, begin with a "Well, er, yes . . ." If he is diffident about his own judgement, he may continue ". . . because it seems to me that . . ." and then pause to choose between such alternatives as "what you have said", "your suggestion", or "your proposition" before deciding on the latter. Then, conscious of the fact that he intends to side with one member of the group against another, and wishing to be tactful, he may hesitate, fill the pause with something like, "as it were" or "you see", and end with "meets the case better than Jack's". Thus, what he comes out with in the end may be something like, "Well, er, yes, I agree, because it seems to me that your er proposition, as it were, meets the case better than Jack's."

He will, by now, be aware of the effect of what he is saying on the rest of the group, and this awareness will inevitably have its impact on what he then goes on to say. He finds himself under constant

129

pressure to revise what he is saying as he goes along, perhaps to blur the impact of what he is saying by disguising his meaning, his feelings, his attitudes, with apologetic disclaimers like "if you see what I mean", as well as common fillers such as "well" and "er". In other words, his own response to the effect that his words are having on others will lead him continually to modify his decisions about what to say next. What he says is the product of rapidly made, and rapidly modified, decisions, as he calls upon the store of language in his brain to meet the demands of the situation.

The injunction to "Spit it out, then", sometimes given to a man hesitating as to what to say next, is based upon the same kind of misconception about the planning and production of speech as underlies the folk-linguistic notion of fluency in speech. This folk-lingistic notion of spontaneous speech (spontaneous, as opposed to prepared and rehearsed in the form of a lecture or speech in a debate) conceives of fluent speech as continuous stretches of sound which are producing long, grammatically perfect sentences. If the speaker is not 'fluent' then he will be interrupting the flow of his sentences by pauses and what are popularly known as 'ums' and 'ers'. But this picture of spontaneous speech is based upon an illusion in the same way as, in the cinema, the illusion of continuous moving pictures is produced by a rapid succession of images and split seconds of darkness. The rapid succession of sound and silence which, in fact, constitutes speech may be demonstrated by converting speech into a visual record, for example on an oscillograph, where the separate bursts of sound can be seen moving across the screen or recorded on paper.

The ratio of sound to silence in speech varies from one individual to another, and, within the range of any one individual's speech habits, according to the situation in which he is speaking. The proportion of silence has, in fact, been found to be as much as 40–50% of the total speaking time. Silence is as much a part of the speech act as sound.

The most noticeable silences are those known as hesitation pauses, when the speaker hesitates, like the man in the discussion group, as though searching for what to say. As we have seen, such pauses are sometimes filled with 'ums' and 'ers', sometimes left unfilled. In either case, they are related to the way in which speech is put to-
130

gether from the elements of language stored in the brain. They tend to come at those points where a speaker is choosing what to say next.

In one well-known piece of research, Professor Goldman Eisler tried to evaluate the significance of unfilled pauses occurring before *words* in sentences. She carried out experiments based upon the guessing game devised by C. E. Shannon, which requires the player to guess the words in sentences unknown to him but known to the experimenter. From the number of attempts required to guess each word correctly, it is possible to work out the probability of one word occurring after another in a sentence. This likelihood of occurrence, Shannon called *transition probability*. The easier it is to predict a word, the higher its transition probability and the lower its information content; the more difficult to predict, the lower its transition probability and the higher its information content. If it were necessary to send a telegram expressing regret at being unable to attend a meeting on the following Friday, it would be a matter of economy to say REGRET UNABLE ATTEND MEETING FRIDAY. It would not be necessary to waste money on "I . . . that I am . . . to . . . the . . . on . . ." because, with REGRET UNABLE ATTEND MEETING FRIDAY in front of him, the recipient would be able quite easily to guess the missing words. They have, in Shannon's terms, higher transition probability, and lower information content, than the REGRET UNABLE ATTEND MEETING FRIDAY kind of word, which have higher information content.

Goldman Eisler found that longer pauses tended to occur before words of lower transition probability, that is, before words of greater information content. This suggests that more time is needed to choose them. However, as D. S. Bloomer has pointed out in an article reprinted in the Penguin collection, *Language*, we do not choose and plan what we are going to say word by word. Language, as he says, is the product of "a rather more complex process in which planning ranges forward to encompass a structured 'chunk' of syntax and meaning." The words which we choose to convey our meaning have to be combined in grammatically appropriate chunks. But, wherever they occur, there is no doubt that hesitation pauses are an integral part of the process by which an individual produces language, a process which begins with the choice of elements of language, continues with the planning of these elements into longer stretches, and ends when these longer stretches are uttered as sequences of sounds.

131

Further light is thrown on the nature of this process by the 'mistakes' we are all liable to make from time to time. By 'mistake' is meant those occasions when the speaker recognises that what he actually said was not what he had intended to say. In fact, he may sometimes go on to say, "I mean to say . . .", and go back to 'correct' himself. He may, on the other hand, ignore the 'mistake' and carry on.

Among the most frequent of such 'mistakes' are transpositions, anticipations, repetitions. The best-known examples of transpositions are probably spoonerisms, as in the famous "Kinquering kongs their titles take", where a sound from an early place in the utterance has been transposed with a sound from a later stage. However, whole words may sometimes be transposed, as in "Put never round brackets", instead of "Put brackets round never." Anticipation involves the utterance of a sound, or a word, before the place for which it had been planned; and repetition, the repeating of a word or part of a word. Sometimes, too, what is actually uttered contains evidence that, at some point in the process by which the speaker was deciding how to say what he wanted to say, he was selecting from more than one possibility. Fragments of the discarded choice find their way into the utterance, as in "I were against me . . . my mother and father were against me . . ." or "The fish pan needs frying", when what was meant was "The frying pan needs washing" —because fish had been cooked in it.

Careful listening, either 'live' or to a tape-recording of any spontaneous discussion, will reveal that features like these are part of all spontaneous speech. Under the heading Sloppy English, a daily newspaper printed a letter complaining that a school governor had been heard to say, on the radio, ". . . I had have resigned . . ." The writer's complaint was that this was an example of 'bad grammar' inexcusable in a school governor, when it was no doubt a combination of choices which had presented themselves at an early planning stage.

It is important to recognise the characteristic features of spontaneous speech, the pauses, the 'mistakes', the fillers, for what they are, part of the speech production process. A readiness to tolerate, in others, features which are an integral part of all fluent speech, including one's own, means, in effect, giving to others a better chance of saying what they want to say. This has crucial implications for discussions

132

set up as learning situations, where pupils are given the opportunity to learn by talking about, and listening to others talking about, a new or unfamiliar subject.

2

"Stop asking questions. Just write down what I say."

A teacher enters a class-room and calls for silence. In the popular view, he is putting an end to 'idle chatter' or 'idle gossip' before embarking on the serious business of the lesson. This view underlies the description of 'playground talk' offered by a contributor to a collection of papers on non-specialist English Studies in the Sixth Form published by the General Studies Association some years ago. He described such talk in this way: "The speech habits are not usually those we want to encourage. Often they are merely grunts, the speech is slovenly and slurred . . . and there is little coherence or logical argument in operation." Such views rest on a complete misconception of the nature and function of speech in human society. For one thing they ignore all those purposes to which language is put, discussed in Chapter 3, except the last—language as a means of communicating about something. Of this function, Professor Halliday commented, "This is the only model of language that many adults have; and a very inadequate model it is, from the point of view of the child."

The talk interrupted by the teacher's entrance might just possibly, in a class meeting for the first time, say, at the beginning of a school year, have been serving the purpose simply of preventing silence between people liable to be interpreted as hostile. This is speech acting as what Malinowski called 'phatic communion', by which "ties of union are created by a mere exchange of words".

However, any class or group which has met together several times before will have outgrown the need to engage in conversation to relieve awkwardness, or reduce tension by exchanging remarks about the weather or their health. The members of the group will have established relationships with each other, and the maintaining of those relationships requires the use of language. Arrangements need to be made, information exchanged, feelings compared—in short, life has to be lived.

The contribution of any one individual to the aggregate of talk generated by the class as a whole will reflect his participation in the relationship from which a particular conversation derives. How many are there in the small group? What are their relationships with each other? Which of them, if any, is deferred to? What expectations do they have about the use of language in such situations? When, for instance, is it permissible to interrupt someone else's talk? If and when an individual joins in the conversation will be determined by considerations such as these. How he joins in will depend upon the general store of language that he has accumulated, and how much of this he is able to draw upon in a given situation. His 'linguistic biography' will have furnished him with a reservoir of language, and what he actually says in a given period of time will depend upon how he is able to draw upon this to meet the needs of the moment.

If we analyse the kinds of speech being used in a situation like this by reference to the functions listed in Chapter 3 we can see that all may have been in use, somewhere in the class-room, before the teacher entered.

Language as a means of getting on with other people will be required by any group that has to live and work together, while the need to express feelings and attitudes will have required at some time a personal use of language. Someone in authority, a prefect or form-captain, perhaps, may have been trying to reduce the noise, and thus using language—"Don't make so much noise"—to control the behaviour of his class-mates. He may also have been trying to get something done: "Come on, pass your books forward."

Elsewhere, language might have been used to find something out— "What did he set for homework?"—or to communicate something, as in "Learn 'Friends, Romans, countrymen' from *Julius Caesar*." It is also possible, according to the age of the class, that language will have been used for imaginative purposes, such as scurrilous rhymes, or other forms of linguistic humour.

In other words, if we use this analysis of the purposes of language as a yard-stick, all seven might well have been in use before the teacher came into the room. The teacher's entry will change the situation, for he will establish the conditions under which talk can now take place, and define the purposes for which he wishes to encourage talk. His relationship with the class, their relationship with him, their expectations of what he is about to do, will change the constraints operating on the use of language.

He may begin by calling for silence—language to regulate behaviour —before engaging in a form of social, that is inter-actional, talk to re-establish his relationship with the class. This will be relaxed and informal, with no direct pressure exerted on any single member of the class to participate.

A change in the kind of talk may be signalled in a number of ways: by an order ("Open your books at page 95"), by a direct question ("Where did we get to last time, Smith?"), by a general question ("What did I set for homework?"), or even by a non-verbal signal, such as the teacher getting out his own book, or beginning to return corrected work.

A class, if the teacher is well known to them, will have learnt to recognise such signals. They are the precedents by which they judge his expectations and on which they base their response. If he is not known to them, they will have to predict his expectations by reference to similarities they perceive to comparable situations.

He may then begin with an exposition designed to link something new to something that has gone before; that is, language to convey information, the representational function. Listening to this exposition will be a different experience for each member of the class, not only from the acoustic point of view that everybody hears something different because he is sitting differently placed to the source of sound. Essentially, what each member of the class will be trying to do is to match what he hears to his own existing store of language, and so find meaning in what is being said, a process discussed in the previous chapter.

At this stage, it is impossible to tell how well anyone is succeeding, for what is taking place is a private process. This is not the same as saying that it is a passive process, for the attempt to find the language within his own resources that will match what is being said is an active, productive process.

135

A new factor is introduced, however, as soon as he feels obliged to answer a question. It may be directed towards him by name, and formulated in ways that limit the scope of his reply to varying degrees. At one end of the scale a question like "Have you got your book open?" restricts possible answers to 'yes' or 'no'. At the other, a question like "What do you think, Smith?" allows variations of reply. It demands of 'Smith' a greater degree of assessment of what would constitute an appropriate response.

On the other hand, the question may not be directed at any particular person: "Does anybody know . . . ?" or "Who can tell me . . ?" Another factor has thus been fed into the pressures operating upon any one individual's use of language: he has to decide for himself whether he wants to reply or not. Perhaps the teacher requires from his question, ultimately, a specific answer as the bridge to another phase of the lesson. If he does not get what he wants, he may re-phrase his question to try to stimulate the required answer. Such a question and answer session means that the terms on which an individual may participate are narrowly defined. He must accept the formulation of the question, so that his scope for offering an individual contribution is limited.

His chance of doing this may come during another phase of the lesson, to which the question and answer session may have been designed to lead, and which may be signalled by another kind of question, like "What does anybody think . . . ?" Each member of the class now has the opportunity to participate, as it were, on his own terms, yet still within the framework defined by the teacher.

This framework is ostensibly meant to promote the use of language for learning, with the language subject to the teacher's control and direction. It will, like all conversation, be subject to rules, such as those which govern the right to interrupt a speaker. It will probably be conducted on a more formal level than the conversation, reflecting a more formal arrangement of the class, the typical structure perhaps of a learning situation within the school. How far the teacher directs the course of the discussion by interjecting questions, to change its direction or by inviting particular members of the class to make a contribution, will reflect his own view of what constitutes discussion, and what he hopes its product will be. It is more than likely that the aim of any such discussion will be to promote greater familiarity with,

136

and increased ability to handle the language of part of a particular area of knowledge—that part of a subject in the school curriculum, for example, which the class has just reached. The possibility of an individual making a contribution in such a situation will be limited by his familiarity with the language being used. This, in turn, will depend upon the starting-point, its relationship to his existing knowledge and experience, and the expectations of the teacher about the appropriacy of the language to the age of the class. Such expectations will reflect the language he habitually uses to discuss particular areas of his subject, including what he judges to be a level of abstraction appropriate to a particular class.

By listening to the contribution others make to the discussion, even if he is not ready to contribute himself, a member of the class will be familiarising himself with the language. In any case, the possibility of individual contributions to a discussion in a class of, say, thirty, sitting at desks in rows of six, is limited. If every member of the class were called upon to say something in the course of a forty-minute period, individual contributions would be limited to about a minute each.

One method of ensuring greater possibility of individual contribution is to divide the class into groups of five or six for small-group discussions. This has other advantages. The seating can be arranged so that every member of the group can see everybody else face-to-face. In such small groups, a relationship can be set up which results in individuals feeling under less pressure, and therefore more ready, to make contributions. They may be more willing to tolerate in themselves, as well as in others, those features we have seen to be characteristic of all spontaneous speech, and thus more willing themselves to venture a contribution.

The point reached by each group when the discussion has to stop may be reported to the whole class, and short class discussion can try to pull the group discussions together. Each member of the class will, in this way, have been exposed to, and been given the chance to, contribute to talk at a number of levels.

All this is far removed from the 'stop asking questions—just write down what I say" approach. It has regard to the way in which language actually works, within and between people. It recognises

137

that language performs many functions, often at the same time, even though the chief concern of the teacher is with Halliday's *representational* model. But, here again, we have to acknowledge the fact that, if pupils are to reach out from their own language towards a new, if —to adapt G. H. Lewes' phrase—new language is to be soluble in the old, then they must have the chance to match what they hear with their own store of language, so that they may find meaning in it. By creating appropriate conditions, those whose job it is to set up learning situations can maximise the pupils' chances.

REFERENCES

1. Speech.
D. S. Boomer, "Hesitation Pausing and Grammatical Encoding" in *Language*, ed. R. C. Oldfield and J. C. Marshall (Penguin).
F. Goldman Eisler, *Psycholinguistics* (Academic Press, N.Y.).
D. B. Fry, "Speech Reception and Perception" in *New Horizons in Linguistics*, ed. J. Lyons (Pelican).
M. A. K. Halliday, *Intonation and Grammar in British English* (Mouton).

2. Talk.
M. L. Johnson Abercrombie, *The Anatomy of Judgement* (Pelican).
D. Barnes, "Language in the secondary class-room" in *Language, the learner and the school*, D. Barnes and J. Britton (Penguin).
D. Barnes, "Classroom Contexts for Language and Learning" in *The Context of Language* (Educational Review, Vol. 23, No. 3, 1971).
C. Hannam, P. Smyth and N. Stephenson, *Young teachers and reluctant learners*, Chapter 6 (Penguin).

Nine   Spoken and written

1

This chapter explores the nature of spoken language as an objective view sees it, looks at the nature of writing, and sets out some of the main differences between spoken and written language.

There is a story of an ancient culture where travellers of a certain class were accustomed to show courtesy to their hosts by playing chess with them. By the custom of the country, each player used his own set of chessmen. One visitor brought out his own set of crudely carved, unpainted pieces, and set them before his host's set of finely carved and valuable ivory. The onlookers laid their usual bets on the result, and most of them backed the player with the ivory pieces. To their surprise, they lost their money, and however many times they backed the player with the ivory pieces, nine times out of ten they would lose their money. The moral of this fable is that we are apt to make rather similar mistakes about speech. We tend to be more impressed by the speaker with a finely carved accent, forgetting that, whatever the pieces may look like, whatever the accent may sound like, the participants are playing the same game, speaking the same language, following rules just as complicated.

Of all the 'elements and structure' which make up language, the sounds of speech are the most fundamental. Sounds convey meaning because we use them in regular patterns which all the speakers of a language know intuitively. Human beings are capable of making a great many sounds with their speech-organs, very many more than in any particular language they actually use. Another way of putting this is to say that any particular language uses only a small selection of the total number of possible sounds. And languages vary in the selections they use, as we can see by comparing languages. English, for example, does not use the final sound in the French *aiguille*, the heavy aspiration in Dutch that is written as *g* at the beginning of *guilder*, or the cluster of consonants in the middle of the German *Mädchen*. Because these are outside the *sound-system* of English, they sound foreign to us and may be difficult to learn. In the same way, there are sounds in the English system which are difficult for foreigners—the consonant sound in *the* is a well-known instance. Going beyond Europe involves us in a much wider range of

139

speech-sounds, and some Asian languages have sound-systems which have very few sounds in common with the speech-sounds of European languages.

The sounds of speech can be meaningful only if they happen in regular patterns. This is true of most human activities: you cannot be a good footballer until you know how all the other players will operate and until you know the complete set of rules which allow you to predict what they might do and cannot possibly do. Again, a particular musical note is meaningful only because it exists in meaningful patterns of contrast, not merely to other notes, but to other notes in the same key, to similar notes in other keys, and to patterns such as sharp and flat, piano and forte, and so on. So, too, with language sounds: *pin* differs from *bin*, and from all the other English words which consist of an initial consonant followed by /i/ and /n/.

A sound which is the only point of difference between two otherwise similar words is thus *contrastive*: it alone makes the contrast between the two. In that sense, then, the initial consonants of *pin* and *bin* are contrastive. The same holds for the initial consonant sounds in these words:

tin   din   kin   chin   gin   fin   thin   sin   shin   win.

The contrastive consonant sounds in this set bring us to twelve basic sounds. By taking a different set of sounds as the frame, we get some more:

get   let   net   met   yet   vet.

A further group appears in

heal   real   zeal

and there are three other consonant sounds in English English, found in the middle of *leisure*, at the start of *then*, and at the end of *sung*.

The basic consonant sounds of the language thus total twenty-four. We could follow a similar process of working out the basic vowel sounds, but readers may like to do this for themselves. It cannot be done with accuracy in writing unless phonetic notation is used, and this book has been written without this. Unlike the consonants as a

140

whole, too, the vowels of English vary a great deal from region to region, different accents using slightly different numbers of vowels. North-eastern speech, for example, does not use the long /a/ of the southerner's pronunciation of *castle*: the vowel in the northerner's *bar* is slightly different, and his pronunciation of *castle*, with a short a, is quite different. For standard English speech, however, there are twenty-four basic vowel sounds, which can be studied in more detail in the book on which this account has been largely based, Gimson's *Introduction to the Pronunciation of English*. These forty-four sounds are basic in the sense that they are contrastive: any two meaningful sets of sounds, which differ in respect of only one of the sounds, will differ in meaning.

Forty-four is a very small number of sounds, considering what language can do with them. But the *sound-system* (technically the phonology) of a language consists of much more than the basic sounds themselves. It also includes the combinations which can be made with them—and the number of combinations possible with forty-four items is enormous. This power of combination is what makes it possible to make do with so small a set of sounds. But there are two difficulties. First, can we say that the Londoner's word *button*, with a glottal stop in place of the /t/, and the Ulsterman's word *button*, with its soft /t/, are both using the same basic sound? Secondly, the sound we represent in writing as *t* can sound very differently in different situations: the words *metal, beaten, lighter,* and *battery* present four slightly varying spoken versions of the sound. Can we really say that all four (and several other variants) belong to the same basic sound?

The 'basicness' of the forty-four basic sounds derives, not from the fact that every speaker always uses all of them, but from a rather more abstract point. After all, the Ulsterman knows where the Londoner is using a sound belonging to the same family as his own /t/, and vice-versa, and both know when a 'posh' speaker is doing so. All three speakers know intuitively that these slightly varying uses of the basic /t/ sound have some common property, though it might be hard to say what it was. The same is true in music: many different hearers would recognise the note *doh* in its several possible differences of pitch according to key, would recognise the same note whatever octave it was played in, and would also recognise it whatever the timbre of the instrument it was played on. Linguists have found it useful to have a name for this rather abstract conception of a speech-sound which in actual speech can have any of a number of particular sounds: they call it a *phoneme*. That is, the phoneme /t/ is not itself a particular sound in the cluster or family of related sounds which make up the phoneme. Rather, it is a useful abstraction, a way of looking at sounds. The particular sounds we speak and hear will be realisations of the phoneme.

The particular sounds within the family labelled as a phoneme will vary in several ways. One kind of variation is, as suggested, according to region: it is because the particular sounds which a regional accent uses, within several phonemes, are distinctive in broadly similar ways that we recognise it as an accent. Another way has to do with the formality or otherwise of a speaker's use of language. If you ask for the butter at a polite dinner party your /t/ is likely to be rather more noticeable than when you do so at your own breakfast-table. But a more important way in which sounds within a phoneme can vary has to do with the phonemes immediately round it. There is a difference, for example, between /t/ after a long vowel (*beaten*) and /t/ after a short one (*bit*), or between /t/ before a vowel and /t/ before another consonant (as in *term* and *bottle*). If one wanted to be much more subtle one could consider also whether there may not be shades of difference in a consonant phoneme occurring after different vowels, as in *bit, beat, boot, foot, hat*, etc.

The phoneme is thus, in effect, a family of closely related sounds, and its essence is that it isn't any other phoneme. Most speakers of a language can and do use the full range of phonemes which make up its sound-system, as well as many of the variations which can occur within each one. The reader will be able to work out some examples of the kinds of combinations of phonemes which are frequent in English, as well as the kinds which the sound-system of English does not allow. It is the combination-rules of our language which tell us that some sound-patterns are foreign in origin, whether English has adopted some of them as borrowings or not. Borrowed examples include *spaghetti* but not *gnocchi*, *unique* but not *sliwowitz*, *Madras* but not *Phnom-Penh*.

One of the regular patterns of combination which the folk-linguistic of many people embraces is, of course, the syllable. There is no simple way of defining this, beyond saying that it almost always has a vowel at its most prominent point, often with a consonant before and after it. The vast majority of English syllables fall into the three patterns of Consonant + Vowel (e.g. *too, by, no*), Vowel + Consonant (*inn, eat, is*), or Consonant + Vowel + Consonant (*bat, tune, ream*). Parents telling their children about words often divide words up into syllables quite naturally, and this sort of knowledge is a good example of the knowledge OF language referred to at the beginning of Chapter 2.

2

The difference between spoken and written language might, at first glance, seem very obvious. Speech is rapid while writing is slow. Speech is transient while writing is, or can be, permanent. Speech is usually addressed to persons face-to-face while writing is usually addressed to a distant audience. But, as earlier chapters have suggested, there are many differences between spoken and written language. It is not just that we choose one or the other, according to the situation we are in: which one we choose will have some effect, and may have very marked effect, on the language we go on to use.

First of all, speech possesses a number of features which are not available to writing, and in fact relies quite heavily on them. Voice-quality, the emotional colouring of utterances, the placing of casual or intentional pauses, the posture of the body, the gestures of the hands, the expression of the face, contact between eyes, and the like, all play some part and contribute to its greater flexibility. As we have seen in Chapter 5, speech makes possible a freedom in the taking up of roles, and a subtlety in relationships, which may be very difficult to secure in writing. In his mother tongue a speaker makes full use of this freedom and is very sensitive to it in the speech of others. This is one reason why spoken language is not like written text: ordinary conversation, when written out verbatim from a recording, will look quite different from the dialogue of a novelist. There may well be much less of the grammatical error, false-starts, or illogicality that have been attributed to spoken conversations by some writers, but the spoken conversation of ordinary people who know one another well is bound to be obscure to the outsider, to make use of the common stock of family or group knowledge, history, experience, and so on. The writer of dialogue for stage or page has to be much more explicit. Similar considerations apply, for example, to the contrast between the talk of a commercial office and the language of business letters.

Where speech and writing do *not* differ, however, is in the way which a book-based education may lead many Englishmen to suppose: it cannot necessarily be said that written language is somehow more correct than spoken language. For each of the many diverse ways of speaking English in England can be found, on inspection, to have its own distinctive set of speech-sounds which do not correspond to conventional notions of correctness. There is scarcely a speaker of English, however 'posh' or 'cultured', whose normal speech does not offer speech-sounds which some linguistic purist would object to. Our folk-linguistic tells us that the only speakers who 'drop' sounds in their speech are those who talk about "goin' 'ome to 'ave 'is tea". But our folk-linguistic has filtered out from our attention that even the 'poshest' speaker of English quite normally 'drops' the /t/ in saying "I don't know", and equally normally runs together sounds which in written form look distinct. This latter process of *assimilation* is very widespread in English speech, and is just as common at all levels in the social scale. Gimson, in his *Introduction*, lists several hundred examples of it, such as these:

the /d/ in *good girl* is spoken as a /g/,
the /n/ in *ten Players* is spoken as /m/,
the /t/ in *that cup* is spoken as /k/,
the /t/ in *that pen* is spoken as /p/.

A similar process known as *elision* leads to the omission of the *a*'s in *go and get another*, or the /k/ in *asked them*. These patterns are normal, not only in the ordinary speech of people of all classes, but even in the speech of quite formal utterance—as close attention to any sermon or news bulletin will reveal.

These instances of linguistic reality differ from our folk-linguistic very much as do the patterns of continuous speech described in Chapter 8, but they do not equal in importance the role of *intonation* in the difference between spoken and written language. In this context, intonation is a technical term, meaning something more precise than 'the way we say things'. It refers to three distinct aspects of speech, in each of which it works in regular, patterned ways

144

which are closely related: stress, pitch, and what can be called the 'chunking' of what we say.

The best known of these is probably *stress*, the choice of which word or syllable in a group of words is to have the strongest emphasis. This, in turn, implies that speech falls into groups of words, or chunks, each one of which will have a main point of stress. Thus, "I want to go *home*" is one chunk with one stress, but the stress could be different—"I *want* to go home" or "*I* want to go home". But the utterance "I want to go home and get Jim's supper ready for when he comes in" will probably fall into three chunks with one stress in each, "I want to go *home* / and get Jim's *supper* ready / for when he comes *in*". The chunking of what we say is itself something we can choose: one could well say "I want to *go—home*!", as two chunks, the second consisting of only one syllable.

While the placing of stress is also something we can choose, the mere fact of emphasis is not the whole story either. We can choose the pitch of our stress—whether to place it high, middle, or low to begin with; and we can choose the direction in which the pitch changes—whether rising or falling. Change of pitch is an aspect of intonation which contributes to meaning in speech quite as much as the location of stress or the chunking of utterance. If one says to a friend "You want to go *home*", with the stress on the last word, even quite a light stress, whether one is making a statement or asking a question depends entirely on the pitch of the speaker. A choice of medium pitch followed on the stressed word by a rising pitch will at once be taken as a question. A choice of high pitch, with a fall on the stressed word, will be taken as a statement which invites confirmation. A choice of middle pitch, with a moderate fall on the stressed word, will be taken as a simple statement of fact or a stating of an obvious truth. With the stress on other words in the utterance these and other possible choices of pitch will have specific meanings which the competent speaker/hearer of the language knows intuitively.

Describing changes of pitch with any accuracy in writing is virtually impossible: it needs a notation, just as music does, and it would take too much space here to set one up for the purpose. In any case, there are two examples readily available which do this well, and the reader who wants to pursue intonation in any detail should consult

145

O'Connor and Arnold's textbook or the relevant parts of the OUP *Course in Spoken English*, both listed in the bibliography.

The intonation patterns of spoken English supply us with a wide but very precise set of ways of expressing particular meanings—statements, questions, commands, exclamations, threats, and qualified forms of these. Moreover, these patterns operate on a wide variety of actual sentences in much the same way. Thus, in the utterances "*You* want to go home", "*I*'ve been rather a fool", "*He*'s not as good as he thought", and many others, a pitch-pattern which starts fairly high, shows a sharp fall on the stressed word, followed by a gradual slow rise at the end, will convey the meaning of a rueful admission of the truth. The competent speaker/hearer knows these patterns intuitively, and as Chapter 3 suggests, we probably learn the meanings conveyed by intonation patterns before we know the actual words.

The range of intonation-patterns is very considerable. This is because it uses several variables at once: we can choose between small and large changes of pitch, between upward and downward movements of pitch, between high-, middle- and low-pitched starting-points, as well as the more complicated but still regular patterns of falling-and-rising or rising-and-falling pitch. This range is available over and above the possibilities offered by word-order and word-choice, and the language makes very full use of them.

Particular situations sometimes lead to intonation-patterns which become so habitual as to be immediately recognisable. Auctioneers, for example, sometimes have a distinct set of intonations for use at the rostrum, as also do some sports commentators. Clergymen are prone to clerical intonations as well as to distinctive voice-quality. These characteristic intonations occur because the meanings which they convey are frequent in the language of the users. But this does not mean that clergy or auctioneers cannot use the ordinary range of patterns like anyone else.

With some of this range set out in a more orderly way, the reader can work out some of the pitch-patterns involved:

Utterance + Stress	Implication
Joe bought that new car yesterday.	It was Joe rather than Jack.

Joe *bought* that new car yesterday	1. Rather than looking further, *or* 2. as you expected he would, *or* 3. contrary to your expectation.
Joe bought *that* new car yesterday.	Rather than this one here.
Joe bought that *new* car yesterday.	Rather than the second-hand one.
Joe bought that new *car* yesterday.	And not the fancy motor-cycle.
Joe bought that new car *yesterday*.	1. And see what a mess it's in now, *or* 2. Rather than doing it next week, *or* 3. And acts as if he's always had it.

The same set of words, of course, can express a question:

Joe bought that new car yesterday?	How could he afford it?
Joe *bought* that new car yesterday?	He wasn't on a test drive, then?
Joe bought *that* new car yesterday?	Did you know what a fool he's been?

As we have seen, the statements will be marked by a falling pitch on the stressed word, while the questions will have a rising pitch on it. The degree of rise in the pitch will indicate whether the question is seeking information, expressing disbelief, or making a joke. But the change of pitch on the stressed word may be accompanied by other, associated rises and falls elsewhere in the chunk, which will modify the over-all meaning. Meanings which can be conveyed in this way, by the same string of words, would include:

He wasn't just looking at it—he was really serious.
He's got a lot more (or less) taste in cars than we thought . . .
We were kidding him about teasing the dealer, but . . .

Naturally, such subtle variations will often convey meanings which can be understood only by knowing some tiny detail in the recent history of the participants or their conversation—a detail which no outsider could know. This, in turn, contributes to the extreme economy of expression that spoken language is capable of.

3

Spoken language works by its use of a sound-system made up of phonemes and the ways in which phonemes can be combined. Written language works by its use of a writing-system, made up of symbols and the ways in which symbols can be combined. But English uses *orthographic symbols* which are much more numerous than the letters of the alphabet. This arises because letters can be combined into two-letter and three-letter symbols. Thus, we have *c*, and *h*, but also *ch*. We have *d*, and *g*, and *dg*, usually written as *dge*. Beyond this, the writing-system furnishes additional symbols by making some of them do double duty, or, in fact, act as two different symbols in different situations. Thus, *y* at the end of a word is a symbol for the /i/ phoneme, as in *daily*, but at the start of a word symbolises the /j/ phoneme, as in *yacht*. Consistently with this, one phoneme may have more than one symbol according to its position in a word: the two consonants in *judge* are the same phoneme. In these complex ways the writing system is able to solve the problem of representing many more phonemes than there are letters in the alphabet.

However, the correspondences between sound and symbol which make up the writing-system are rather complicated. Before they had been given a reasonably full and accurate description, it was common, and possibly part of our folk-linguistic, to believe that the English writing-system was completely chaotic and in need of radical reform. Suffice it here to say that an adequate reform of the writing-system has to meet a very diverse set of criteria if it is to be any improvement on the one we have. Some of these will become apparent in the following pages.

Each of the phonemes of the language is represented in the writing-system by a limited set of corresponding symbols. Which one of this set is used in particular situations will depend on the particular situation, but similar immediate situations tend to produce similar choices of symbols, so that the over-all distribution of symbols is regular. Thus, the consonant in *judge* has three corresponding symbols—*j*, *dg*, *dge*. As the example suggests, *j* is the usual one for this phoneme in initial position of words or syllables (cf. *misjudge*). *dge* is the usual symbol at the end of a word or syllable if the following syllable begins with a consonant (cf. *judgement*). *dg* is used at the end of a syllable before another vowel (cf. *judging*). There are rules governing the choice of symbol which are not solely positional: some relate to the immediately preceding or following symbols. Thus, the /t/ phoneme will be represented by *t* after a single vowel-symbol, as in *bit* or *hut*. But if there is a following syllable the symbol for /t/ will be *t* after a long vowel-sound and *tt* after a short one (as in *biter* and *butter* respectively). Again, this pattern is regular and applies in general to many other consonant phonemes. However, the presence of a choice between symbols presents the opportunity of using different symbols for distinguishing words which sound alike, as we shall see in a moment.

Some phonemes have more symbols available to them than others. The long vowel in *beet* also occurs in *mean* and *scene*, as well as in the rare legal term, *lien*. But the long vowel in *vie* can also be heard in *rye, ride, sign, indict, Blyth, quite, why, buy*. Interestingly, none of these symbols uses *i* on its own for this sound, which seems confined to the first person pronoun and *pi*. This set of symbols includes examples of several apparent paradoxes, the most obvious of which is that there are some circumstances where a consonant symbol is made use of to symbolise a vowel sound—as with the *g* in *sign*. (The reverse also happens: the /k/ and /w/ phonemes appear as *qu* in *quite*, and the *u* is thus, in this particular situation, a consonant symbol.) One of the reasons for this is that *sign* has to be spelled in a way which makes it different (in writing) from *sine*: the words which sound alike are usually contrasted in the writing-system, and such contrasts are a major aspect of the orthography.

Consider the contrasts which the writing-system provides in these pairs: foul/fowl, roll/role, bow/bough. There are hundreds of these *homophones* in English, and a sore trial to schoolboys they are. But they are really less of a difficulty than they seem. Precious few people listening to a sailor will think he is talking about the boughs of his ship, any more than they will think a forester is talking of cutting the bows off a tree. Speech virtually always tells us which of such a pair of words we are hearing, and our brains are in fact programmed to exclude the one we are not supposed to hear: the schemata of vocabulary in our brains see to it that we do not confuse things. The teacher, of course, has a set of schemata which tell him what a pupil's writing is driving at, however often it makes the wrong choice, and if he did not have such a set he would never be able to make any corrections, or indeed spell words himself.

Before the great age of writing dictionaries in the eighteenth century, English writing often used different spellings of words interchangeably, and there was no noticeable body of unintelligible writing as a result. But dictionaries are easier to write if such visual contrasts as doe/dough, rough/ruff, through/threw, borough/burrow are laid down. Each of these many contrasts has to be made with symbols already in use in the writing-system, but the process of codifying them was not carried as far as it might have been, so that we have many words usable in different grammatical functions without any change in spelling—*bows*, for example, being either verb or noun. Certainly there remain illogicalities, but when we consider the range of purposes served by writing and the enormous range of accents which the English writing-system caters for, they appear relatively few. The *its/it's* contrast, like the *their/ they're/ there* confusions, present problems in school, but if they can be kept in proportion, it should be possible to avoid becoming unduly preoccupied with them. The reader who wishes to pursue the questions involved can consult the Teacher's Manual to *Breakthrough to Literacy*, while a much more complete account of the writing-system can be found in K. Albrow's paper listed in the bibliography to this chapter.

The essence of the matter can be summarised by saying that a mastery of a writing-system, which includes the ability to spell, must rest primarily on *visual* schemata (cf. Chapter 4) rather than aural ones. The brain of the young school child needs to be able to make its 'maps' of experience—including maps of how the written language symbolises sounds. This is why there is virtue in extended and extensive reading in junior schools, and why remedial teachers lay great stress on reading being done aloud. The dependence of spelling on visual schemata is what underlies the well-established objection to using mis-spellings-for-correction as a classroom test, since they can generate mis-learnings which prove hard to put right.

The same reasoning leads to the view that trying to improve children's spelling by improving their pronunciation is a fallacious proposal. Even the most 'correct' pronunciation has just as complex a set of correspondence with the writing system as any other pronunciation. There are some howlers, it is true, which might appear superficially to reflect particular ways of saying certain phrases— 'wouldn't of done it' is an instance repeatedly cited in examiner's reports. But children whose natural speech elides the vowel of 'have' in this phrase are usually taught by teachers whose natural speech normally does exactly the same. After all, if spelling were to be improvable by pronunciation, which accent of English would do most to help? If teachers were to take this seriously, they would presumably run the risk of turning children's everyday conversation into the speech-form of Edwardian theatre, or even of having them pronounce the *l* in *talk* and separate the *p* and *h* in *phoney*.

4

Written language cannot make use of the resources which intonation places at the disposal of spoken language. The literary craftsman is often conscious of the problems which this fact poses, and can find ways round it, developing an intricate subtlety of expression which is one of the defining characteristics of literature. But most ordinary people have to be content with written language which is more approximate, or with expressing themselves in writing in such a way that their mastery of the writing-system can handle what they want to convey. However, one feature of writing which ordinary people, as well as specialists, have to come to terms with is punctuation.

In English, punctuation has a different status from spelling, partly because it could not be standardised as spelling was by lexicographers. It is usually treated, and in textbooks for foreign learners is almost always treated, as denoting the main pauses in a text. However, a written text does not, strictly speaking, have pauses at all. In any case, as the last chapter shows, the actual pauses in a piece of spoken language do not necessarily correspond to the points which would be punctuated if the same text were written down. The set of conventions known as punctuation in English derives, in fact, from two systems. One is a set of signals of grammatical structure, but only the full stop has anything like a consistent and unambiguous set of rules, while the uses of the comma are described by some continental textbooks of English as largely arbitrary and unpredictable. The other system, which most textbooks neglect, derives from the intonation of spoken English, and is a set of signals to mark major

151

changes of pitch and the related chunking of the text mentioned earlier. The full-stop is thus both a grammatical marker and a signal of the end of a chunk; the semi-colon and colon may be both, or one or the other; the comma is likewise uncertain, but some writers (and publishing houses) seem to use the comma chiefly as a grammatical signal, while others seem to use it chiefly to point to places where major pitch-changes can be or ought to be inferred. But neither system is fully carried through, and there is much diversity in published texts, as these examples show:

> This lady (the Reading Teacher) was interesting to me, first of all, because she was one of the most serious and self-consciously moralist people whom I have ever known. She was also, by all odds, the most effective and most high-powered of the old-fashioned teachers who were still around. She was—finally—an extraordinarily, if, at times, quite subtly, bigoted woman. At the same time, however, and like many others in America, she considered herself a politically liberal and enlightened person, was shocked by any imputation of prejudiced behaviour, and even spoke at great length, and sometimes without much mercy, of certain of the dishonesties and secret bigotries of others.
>
> Kozol—*Death at an Early Age*, Ch. 3.

> It is possible to gain a better understanding of attempted suicide if we regard it as conveying a particular degree of uncertainty that the attempt will succeed or fail. Attempts at suicide are unlike successful suicides and they are made by different people in different ways. The true goal of the attempted suicide is not self-destruction but survival, without however losing the advantages of self-destruction. The reverie which precedes the suicidal attempt contemplates the possible consequences and concludes that suicide would do more harm than good, and would therefore defeat its own purpose which is often to compel affection and esteem.
>
> Cohen—*Chance, Skill, and Luck.*

In neither of these passages does the punctuation in any significant degree affect the reader's way of apprehending the messages borne by the text, although the apparent weight of the punctuation varies. To the extent that the messages of a text are understandable whichever weight of punctuation an author chooses, we can say that punctuation is to some degree optional. Correspondingly, however, readers vary in their dependence on punctuation. The reader who is accustomed to heavy stopping will not find the punctuation of

Kozol's text at all obtrusive, but may find Cohen's pattern unduly sparse. The reader accustomed to minimise the punctuation will feel the reverse. But what the punctuation is doing in each case is mediating between the written text and the spoken form which the same messages would assume in speech. How much mediation the reader needs may depend on the reader.

This is not, however, the only variable in punctuation. Another is its support, as it were, for the use of written language to do things which spoken language either cannot do or does not usually try to do. For example:

> She could see the words echoing as she spoke them rhythmically in Cam's mind, and Cam was repeating after her how it was like a mountain, a bird's nest, a garden, and there were little antelopes, and her eyes were opening and shutting, and Mrs. Ramsay went on saying still more monotonously, and more rhythmically and more nonsensically, how she must shut her eyes and go to sleep and dream of mountains and valleys and stars falling and parrots and antelopes and gardens, and everything lovely, she said, raising her head very slowly and speaking more and more mechanically, until she sat upright and saw that Cam was asleep.
> Virginia Woolf, *To the Lighthouse.*

Here the punctuation is part of a literary purpose, where the basic patterns are like those of non-literary texts but with special characteristics which vary according to the demands of the text. Even here, however, it is impossible to lay down hard and fast rules about how continuous written text ought to be punctuated which will resolve every doubt and settle every detail. Indeed, the belief that punctuation is subject to rules as strict as those of spelling is part of our folk-linguistic, and the uncertainty which makes our punctuation the flexible thing it can be also makes it a target for those self-appointed guardians of the language discussed in Chapter 2.

The role of intonation as a factor in punctuation of written text has been explored by some teachers in a direct way, by trying to use intonation cues for the purpose of teaching punctuation. The results of their experiments are inconclusive. Certainly, intonation cues can give many students some clues in deciding how to punctuate a written text, but for very many students it is first necessary to master the complex process of matching a written text to the intonations it

153

would receive if spoken. This is in some degree a process of recognising the intonations called for by the way the text is punctuated. The student's difficulties in doing this are increased, not only by the limited experience of reading aloud which he may get in school, but also by the variation in the weight of punctuation found in the written texts he encounters. Further, the student who is made over-anxious about punctuation may learn less than he would otherwise, because what ought to be a process of assimilation has been made into one of conscious learning. For most students, however, punctuation is a minor matter, when weighed against the infinitely more important problems of competence dealt with in Chapter 7.

There is a need for teachers and their pupils to review the prevailing folk-linguistic belief that punctuation follows a single set of obligatory rules. A more constructive approach is to conceive of punctuation as a set of resources from which, in given instances, we can choose. This view will also take account of the evident fact that punctuating practice in written English in our own time is changing very rapidly: the colon and semi-colon have almost disappeared from newspapers and most other non-academic writing, while the dash and the parenthesising pair of dashes have become more common. However, the view of punctuation as a set of possibilities to choose from needs to include 'nothing' as one of the possibilities—as the text quoted from Cohen suggests. It is relatively rarely that a specific stop other than a full stop can be justified solely on grounds of avoiding ambiguity. Teachers, however, are in a slightly special position. They know the art of supplying, for their own understanding, the punctuation which pupils regularly omit from their writing. But this art is the result of long practice, following a long process of internalising the norms of written language in an advanced education through books. The secondary pupil, simply by virtue of being a secondary pupil, still has much of this process to complete, and the middle secondary years present many occasions for that difficult art of doing nothing and waiting.

Bad punctuation and bad spelling often go hand in hand. To many teachers this pattern offers convincing evidence of general linguistic weakness, but the two defects in fact arise from quite different causes. The spelling system and the punctuation of English constitute two quite distinct systems. They are both related to the writing-system, but they relate to quite distinct aspects of the spoken language. The spelling relates to the phonology, through a complex pattern of sound-symbol correspondence, while the punctuation system relates to the intonation system and, in a more intricate way, to the grammatical structure of discourse.

In this connection it is worth noting briefly that a number of aspects of the layout of written text have little or nothing to do with the spelling or punctuation of ordinary prose. The arrangement of a poem, for example, follows a set of conventions about the layout of poems. Relatively few poets go beyond these conventions and bring into their work any exploitation of rules governing orthography or punctuation—e e cummings is celebrated for just this reason. Similarly, printed text has possibilities, not available to the writer of longhand, in the use of multiple type-faces and sizes, columnar layout, and so on, most of which have been exploited for specific purposes, such as the use of italic in an acting edition of a play, or of bold type in the captions for magazine illustrations. In the same way, dialogue in novels and all kinds of letters have conventional patterns of layout which have to be learned. However, some conventions in these matters are more binding than others. It is quite arbitrary to insist that personal letters must be laid out according to the rigid format of business letters: it is equally arbitrary to suppose the layout of a questionnaire or an application form unimportant to its function. The existence of a convention, however, is always liable to generate a body of people for whom the convention seems to matter more than the substance contained within it.

There is good reason why this should be so: communicating needs to take account of the audience being addressed, and some audiences become incapable of receiving if the messages are not couched in the conventional forms. Speech-accent is a common example of this which is discussed in the next chapter: we understand what we know and find difficulty in the unfamiliar. Another example is the case of handwriting. The quotation from Professor Mary Douglas in Chapter 4 applies not only to objects but also to written symbols: "each of us constructs a stable world" in which there are "recognisable shapes. In perceiving, we are building, taking some cues and rejecting others. . . . The most acceptable cues are those which fit most easily into the pattern being built up. Ambiguous ones tend to be treated as if they harmonised with the rest of the pattern." This is precisely what teachers do with written work which is hard to decipher—up to the point at which too many of the cues are ambiguous. When that point is reached, the pupil is told to 'do it again', and the English teacher is blamed for 'declining standards'. For the pupil that point is, in a sense, rather too late to be useful.

Furthermore, handwriting has been the subject of some strange pieces of folk-linguistic. Here again, personal preferences, quite legitimate in themselves, tend to be elevated to the status of law. But the differences between medieval uncial, Victorian copperplate, and contemporary italic, considered as scripts, are very small. Within a wide range of regularity, the legibility of each is a matter of the reader rather than of the writer—as the existence of such alternative orthographies as Greek or Arabic suggest. Once again, the individual pupil is better guided by pragmatic considerations of being legible to wide numbers of readers, than by moralistic assertions that this or that script is 'bad'. Some research work has claimed that examiners can be strongly influenced by the handwriting of the texts they assess, but it is necessary to explore, not merely how different examiners react to a variety of scripts, but also how the same examiners react to a controlled sample of scripts. This would reveal that the judgement of handwriting is as subjective as anyone might expect.

Speech and writing are media, not language. The chessmen are not the game: they do not constitute the rules of the game or the skill of the players, but that is as far as the analogy takes us. The choice of linguistic medium is one of the determining factors in what is said or written.

FURTHER READING

K. A. Albrow, *The English Writing System* in Papers in Linguistics and English Teaching, Series II (Longman).

A. C. Gimson, *An Introduction to the Pronunciation of English* 2nd edn. (Arnold).

D. D. Mackay and B. Thompson, Teacher's Manual to *Breakthrough to Literacy* (Longman).

J. D. O'Connor and G. F. Arnold, *Intonation of Colloquial English* (Longman).

J. McH. Sinclair and M. A. K. Halliday, et al, *Course in Spoken English* (Oxford).

Ten   Accent and dialect

1

Several chapters of this book have explored some of the differences between linguistic reality and our folk-linguistic. Some of the examples of folk-linguistic beliefs quoted earlier throughout this book have been instances of convictions about the social value of our way of speaking. There are a great many beliefs on this subject, and we need to beware of supposing that only other people have misconceptions. We live in a society which is acutely sensitive to variations in accent, with a minutely accurate and delicate sense of social class. It would be unreasonable to expect accent, in these circumstances, to be anything but a very touchy subject.

The purpose of this chapter is to focus on the diversity of modern spoken English, and to draw some useful distinctions about it, suggesting how we might be able to take a more objective view of it. In one sense, of course, this is a very familiar subject: we all know a great deal more about accent, at the intuitive level, than can be written down in a single chapter. Moreover we know it with a sensitivity which cannot even be sought after in a chapter that accepts a basic requirement to avoid using phonetic script. To any reader who has listened and thought about accent in modern England there will be little new in this chapter, but it is just because listening and thinking in an objective way is rather rare that we have to write a chapter about it. The resulting exploration is thus bound to be an instance of the possibly alarming process of transforming the familiar that readers will recognise from earlier chapters. However, the chapter is not saying simply "If you have prejudices, prepare to shed them now". Rather it is asking the reader to consider whether our most intimate attitudes and routine assumptions about speech may not reveal more about those of us who hold them than they tell of language itself.

This is not to suggest for a moment that the differences which form the subject of this chapter are in some way unreal. On the contrary, Scouse and Geordie are different accents and their difference can be assessed in great detail and with considerable physical accuracy. So, too, when a man from Barnsley identifies another man as coming from Bradford, he does it on the basis of describable differences of linguistic substance (among other things, one of the two men pronounces it Bra*t*ford, and so on). In saying that many attitudes to accent are mistaken, it is not being suggested that the accents are somehow illusory, or that they aren't important. Accent must be important, or people would not be so sensitive about it. Some of the reasons for this importance are historical, some social, and some linguistic, and the interested reader who wants to pursue them in greater depth will find an excellent account in Gimson's *Introduction to the Pronunciation of English*.

Consider the word *blood*. In some parts of England it will almost rhyme with *wood*. In other parts it likely to sound very close to *had*. Or take the word *work*: it can range from sounding like the rural Midlander's pronunciation of *Warwick* (as 'Worr'k') to sounding as if it had the same vowel as *there*—and in this case such variation can be found within a space of fifty miles. But whatever variations we find in the regional pronunciations of a word, it is still the same word. So there is a distinction to draw between what is said and how it is said, or, in fine, between *language* and *speech-form*.

Any accent-mimic or impersonator can demonstrate this by saying the same sentence in half a dozen accents in quick succession. The existence of a variety of speech-form in which one language is expressed is a feature of many languages: to most Frenchmen, the French of Provence is strikingly different from that of, say, Bordeaux, and a good ear can tell at once the difference between Geneva French and Dijon French. But it is still the same *language*, however much the *speech-form* may vary. For most of us the chief feature of speech-form is accent, but the term also covers intonation, which may be an important feature of a particular regional speech-form, as in Geordie where a rising intonation at the end of a sentence does not express a question as it does in most other regions. In this chapter the terms *speech-form* and *accent* will be used interchangeably, although the former is technically a wider term.

The existence of variety in the speech-forms of a language is due to history. Dutch is basically a dialect of German, but its differences from German are just as important, linguistically and historically, as its similarities to it. The language of England was a cluster of regional varieties of the same language, of which two can be seen in the work of Chaucer and Langland respectively. Any one of these

158

regional varieties was readily understood by speakers of the neighbouring ones, although speakers from two regions far distant from each other might have difficulty, as in China today. However, over a long period of time there emerged from this collection of related varieties a *standard language* which was understood in all the regions. It is a mistake to suppose that regional varieties of a language develop away from a pre-existing standard: rather, as a language community develops unity and coherence, it also develops a form of the language in which all its members can share. Its chief characteristic, linguistically speaking, is its freedom from words and usages understood only in some regions and not others. But this development is a complicated process: a standard language is much more than the lowest common factor of all the regional varieties.

In the emergence of a standard language, which can take several centuries, many different factors play some part. In England the spread of commerce was interwoven with the influence of the Church and universities and the power of government. In Germany the influence of Luther's Bible was quite certainly powerful, and the English Bibles of Henry VIII's time may have been influential in England. Standard languages also quite naturally show variations in their dependence on particular regional varieties of the language. Standard French naturally reflects Parisian French, since it is the language of a more centralised country than most. In England the south-east and south-midland regions exerted strong influence on standard English, and at a later stage the country's schools played a large part in propagating the standard language, since textbooks were written in it and most teachers spoke it.

However, *standard English* is a language, not a speech-form. There is nothing about standard English which requires it to be spoken with one accent rather than another. British people either speak standard English through having grown up in a home setting where it was the normal language, or speak a regional variety for most of the time. But plenty of standard-English speakers are perfectly capable of speaking a regional variety, and a great many regional speakers can also speak standard English if the need arises. What complicates the situation is that standard English can be spoken in any one of several scores of regional accents: language and accent are not the same.

159

A regional accent, then, is a pattern of sounds which we may hear used by a speaker of a regional variety of the language, or by a speaker of the standard language. Since a speaker may slide from one to the other without any noticeable change in his way of speaking, it may be hard to tell one from the other, and in a social sense this is precisely our intention in making such shifts. An accent is a pattern of speech-sounds, and we have seen that speech sounds exist in families or clusters which in the last chapter were labelled phonemes. In many accents the particular member of one sound-family which is used will be the same one as in other phonemes: one accent will have a general pattern of, for example, vowels spoken well back in the mouth, or of consonants heavily aspirated, and so on. Since these patterns or regional accents are learned when language itself is learned, it is perfectly natural to hear them in both the regional variety and in the standard language as spoken in the same region. So there are many phonetic features of Gaelic which can be heard in Highland Scots, and many of the characteristic sounds of other regional accents can be traced a long way back to before the emergence of the standard language.

Thus far no reference has been made to dialect. One of the reasons is that linguists themselves have not been consistent about its meaning. Another is that where the term does have a clear meaning, it conflates language and speech-form in a way which this section has been seeking to unravel. To the layman, a dialect is any very markedly distinctive way of using language, which may cover both a particularly strong accent and the use of words or grammatical patterns not found in the standard language. To some linguists the term dialect refers simply to the way language varies from region to region—and if the only variation is in accent, then in that instance dialect and accent are the same thing; if there is variation in vocabulary as well, then dialect and accent are different things. Here the term dialect is avoided in order to avoid just that kind of confusion: in keeping with the distinction between language and speech-form, this chapter will distinguish between *standard* and *non-standard language.*

This does not mean that the serious professional study of dialect can be set aside: merely, it uses terms in a slightly different way. Such study is fascinating in its own right, and a great deal of energy has gone into it. One of the most readily accessible examples of its findings

160

can be found on pp. 122–3 of the *Readers Digest Atlas of Great Britain*, which reproduces some of the thousands of distribution-maps that have traced how words and word-usage occur about the country. Even here, however, confusion occurs: most of the captions use *dialect* to mean a regional variety, yet in one of them the accent of public-school boys is also described as a dialect, implying that it, too, is a non-standard language.

2

Non-standard English is thus a term referring to varieties of the language—in grammar or vocabulary—which do not have national currency. *Bairn*, for example, is restricted to the north, and in most parts of the country today it would be thought more than odd to say *housen* instead of *houses*. Any region of the country has its own considerable set of these forms, one or two of which may have become more widely known as typical of the region (like *bairn*, or *wake* in the sense of holiday). But it would probably be a mistake to think of users of regional forms as particularly self-conscious about them. (Some of them may have been *made* self-conscious about them by their schooling, but that is another matter.) A large number of people who speak regional forms of the language at home are perfectly capable of speaking the standard language in circumstances which call for it. The whole point about such switching is the natural and intuitive ease with which it occurs, in response to the speech situations which arise.

For example, the Lancashire man who has grown up speaking a Lancashire non-standard form of the language, and has moved by education or career into situations where the standard language is spoken, will have acquired the standard language—probably with a Lancashire accent. If he then goes to work in London for twenty years he may well lose a good deal of this accent. But if he returned for a visit to his old haunts it would be surprising if he did not 'pick it up again', possibly with some delay during which he would hear a lot of comment on his changed accent. Indeed, *not* to resume his native accents might make his former acquaintances and friends think he was stand-offish, and in a sense they would be right: by not doing the 'natural' thing, he would be refusing to identify himself with his own folk. The same would apply to any regional speaker returning to a former home region.

With the related situation of a school-child who moves from one distinct speech-region to another, we would expect to find problems of adjustment, not only for the newcomer, but also for both his new schoolmates, and, more importantly, for his teachers, whose willingness to give the newcomer time to adjust can contribute to his acceptance by the group. The ridicule which can sometimes be meted out to a speaker of an unfamiliar accent is in one sense a natural reaction against the alien, but to an alien who cannot help his position it must at times seem cruel. Such a situation illustrates yet again the principle that a person's way of speaking is a sign of his loyalties, a marker of those with whom he chooses to group himself, a very audible declaration of his social identity. Where these identifications are very localised, adjusting to new ones may be painful and often have to do with the simplest of everyday things. After all, standard English speakers *make* the tea, but in a belt from Oxfordshire to Suffolk, including most of London, non-standard speakers *brew* it, while Devonians *soak* it and all other southerners *wet* it. In the north, though, they *mash* it, and in the Midlands *brew* and *mash* seem almost interchangeable. Again, most inhabitants of the south-west, from mid-Somerset westwards, tend to pronounce /f/ and /v/ as 'varmer' and 'veet'. Very few visitors to the south-west would stop to think of such usage as 'wrong', and at an earlier period the standard language borrowed the south-west's form for a female fox ('vox'—vixen). But the movement of people between regions can cause real personal distress because speech is so intimately bound up with belonging, and even the most broadminded can sometimes make unwitting blunders.

One reason for this situation is that our folk-linguistic tells us that *non-standard* somehow means *sub*-standard. Most of us have undergone a sustained process of education by teachers who have believed that success in life depended, to some extent, on speaking 'good' English. They defined 'good' as having two features which in their minds hung together: being standard as distinct from non-standard, and being non-regional in accent as distinct from regional. It is only natural that most of us have grown up assuming that one can't speak standard English unless one speaks a non-regional accent, and that to have a regional accent means speaking non- (or sub-) standard English. A moment's thought tells us that this is a nonsense: plenty of American professors speak standard English in a (to us) non-standard accent. This is only one of many examples of the distinc-

162

tions between language and accent. But in England more than in any other English-speaking country accent is a matter of prestige, and this does not fit easily into the pattern of standard and non-standard language.

3

The language habits of many advanced countries include an element of seeking to get rid of regional character from speech. England seems to exhibit a peculiarly marked form of this urge, so that it has a particular speech-form which is variously known, according to the point of view, as 'educated English', 'talking posh', 'an Oxford accent', and so on. This prestige form of spoken English is known among linguists as Received Pronunciation, or RP for short, and Abercrombie's *Studies in Phonetics & Linguistics* contains a very readable account of it. RP emerged in the English ruling class in the Jacobean period, probably originating in the court and strongly supported by the influence of the capital. For some decades it seems to have been regarded as inherently an affectation, as it still is by some people.

RP is important enough in English social history to have had a hand in some noticeable developments. The sudden growth of private boarding schools between 1840 and 1870 was in part due to the pressing desire of newly rich people to equip their sons with RP. This accent was one of the unspoken but powerful defining features of a 'gentleman' as Victorian England understood it. The influence of RP is still very strong—strong enough for it to be regarded, even now, as necessary for certain occupations and, in some quarters, as automatically desirable for social relations. It is strong enough, too, for some students to signal their unrest by refusing to speak it.

However, RP is neither as uniformly admired throughout the country, nor as stable over time, as might be supposed. The mid-Victorian RP-speaker always dropped initial *h*'s, as in *hotel* and *history*—a pattern some can recall in the speeches of Churchill. In genteel circles in the 1870's it was usual to rhyme *Calais* with *palace*, and *Prague* with *Haig*. *Rhyme* would sound remarkably like *same*, and *girl* was indeed *gel*. These pronunciations would today sound like a comic turn, and the accent which Eliza set out to learn in *Pygmalion*, if it were accurately portrayed on the stage today, would sound insufferably la-di-da. Today's RP, on the other hand, would strike a Victorian purist as positively 'low'. One factor in these changes is of course that RP is now the ordinary speech of a much larger proportion of the population than a century ago. One would expect, too, that the narrower gap between the ends of the social scale (whether real or only apparent) is accompanied by a less marked distinctiveness of speech among RP-speakers. What used to be a possibly self-conscious mark of a tiny, privileged élite has become more widely diffused. Indeed, it may be that the social distinctions which RP used to signalise are not as sharp as accent-differences would lead us to think.

There are, too, many variant forms of RP: it is not the sharply defined accent that the label may suggest. On the contrary, while some may speak an RP in which no regional element can be heard, many (perhaps most) RP-speakers have some regional colouring. Many others are evidently capable of shifting fairly readily in and out of a regionally coloured RP. Interestingly, the broadcasting media have kept in step with the changing situation: the BBC's committee on pronunciation no longer lays down laws on the speaking of standard English, and newscasters and weather forecasters are permitted a much wider range of accent than formerly. The purist element in society naturally feels betrayed by this realism, since the defenders of RP in its purest form believe in the power of an accent to alter or control the language spoken in it, a belief which, as we have seen, has no basis in reality.

There are not a few teachers who share this belief, and who sometimes seek to include elocution or good speech in the school curriculum. Very few schools have ever given it the status of a full curriculum subject, which suggests that they do not have much faith in its effectiveness or, more likely, its value to the children. Most teachers know quite well that school-based attempts to 'improve' or 'correct' non-RP speech forms can succeed only if the pupils concerned want them to succeed, and they very seldom do. There is a very good reason why the children should reject such an approach: a child's accent, like an adult's, defines his membership of a social group. To want to alter it implies a rejection of the group. For a teacher to try to alter it implies a threat to the social fabric of the child's life.

However, schools and teachers exert pressure on their pupils' accents
164

in less formal ways than by speech training. Schools are often careful to give public roles to pupils who speak RP, and many discussions in staff rooms about who should become head boy have turned on this issue. Teachers and parents also share the folk-linguistic which believes that RP is in some direct way beneficial to a pupil in purely academic respects. This belief confuses language and speech-form in a way which this chapter's distinction between them has shown to be open to question. But that is not quite the whole story, because there is now good evidence of the power of teachers' expectations to influence their pupils' attainment (well summarised by Pidgeon)—and accent plays a definite part in how those expectations are formed. Frederick Williams reports a series of studies, including some of his own, which investigated teachers' judgements of pupils, and especially the different factors which led to them. These studies found very strong evidence that teachers' judgements of their pupils' dispositions and prospects are influenced by the pupils' accent. It seems that many teachers have a very clear stereotype of the sort of accent to be expected in pupils who are going to do well. It is thus possible that the accent-attitudes of teachers, which can often become apparent to their pupils, play some part in the process which leads children to set themselves high or low standards of attainment in school. Keddie describes some aspects of this process in illuminating detail.

This is *not* quite the same thing as saying that teachers are snobs about accent. In any case, overt pressure on pupils to conform to RP is much less than it used to be, at least in England. But we have to live with the consequences of a period in which non-prestige accents were subjected to sustained disparagement by many adults. To have one's natural way of speaking disparaged by adults is bound to be discouraging, and it would strain probability to expect such feelings not to be reciprocated. There are therefore many sections of English society where RP may be a distinctly unwelcome way of speaking. Further, there are many clues in the recent spate of sociological studies of schools, such as Hargreaves, Lacey, or Jackson & Marsden, which suggest a fairly general working-class hostility to RP as the accent of 'them'. Some teachers have discovered, to their surprise, that pupils who have experienced RP *solely* through the media or from teachers simply cannot believe that RP is ever a native accent: they regard it as inherently a learned or acquired accent, and therefore see it as an affectation.

For this kind of reason, and because different accents make widely differing uses of intonation, pausing, and voice-quality, it is unwise to assume that where a class and their teacher have different accents, both sides will always understand each other straight away. Parity of esteem between accents is nearer than it once was, but we are still a long way from achieving it. As long as attitudes to accent remain emotionally active, difficulties in mutual understanding will remain possible.

4

Peter Doughty has suggested that standard and non-standard *language* and prestige and non-prestige *accent* can vary independently. This brings to our attention the point that RP is by no means the only prestige accent in English. There are thus four possible combinations to listen for:

A. Standard language with prestige accent.
   The educated RP speaker from southern England is the obvious case, but many Scots accents have prestige all over the country too, and where non-standard Scots vocabulary is not used they would be in this category.
B. Standard language with non-prestige accent.
   An educated Yorkshireman, for example. But this combination would also be found in an Indian whose mother tongue was the distinctive form of English which almost became standard in India.
C. Non-standard language with prestige accent.
   The Scot, again, illustrates this, if his speech includes Scottish dialect words. For many large sections of the population, too, pop-group Merseyside has high prestige but is not usually standard English.
D. Non-standard language with non-prestige accent.
   In contrast to most Scots, indigenous working-class Glaswegian speech lacks prestige and has many dialect features. Urban accents generally in England lack prestige, but where Black Country speech tends to be dialectal (i.e. non-standard), many Birmingham accents would belong under B.

English presents a further complication, however, in that there are several English-speaking countries in each of which there is a
166

Standard English peculiar to that country. American English is a standard language. Australian English is likewise a standard language. In England we hear Standard English, but we may also hear many other Englishes which, though standard languages in their own domains, are non-standard in this country. While there are regional variations within many of these standard languages, and some forms have more prestige than others, none of them has a distinct non-regional prestige accent as we have in RP.

Some areas have had particularly complex linguistic histories which have left complex patterns behind. In the West Indies, for example, there is a standard language, West Indian English. There are other patterns which can be confused with it, however. When a community comes into contact with another language for trade purposes, and uses part of it in the course of trading, the result is what is termed a *pidgin*. It is characterised by a small vocabulary and an extreme simplification of the range of sounds used. But when trading foreigners settle, and the native population learns their language well (but far from perfectly), the native children may acquire the resulting learned language as their *native* tongue. Elements of the pre-existing native language are likely to be fused with this, and the result of this process is termed a *Creole* language. There are thus many pidgins and many Creole languages, but where a pidgin is a medium of contact only, a Creole is a language in its own right. West Indians may speak the standard language (which is different from standard (English) English or they may speak a creolised form of English, and specialists in the teaching of immigrants have learned to distinguish one from the other with some care.

The ordinary Englishman who comes into regular contact with Indian or West Indian English finds it no more difficult to become familiar with them than he does with American English or with a very different accent from his own country. All of these have their distinctive patterns of pronunciation and intonation, and learning to recognise them is, from a linguistic point of view, little more difficult than for a Londoner to become at home with Tyneside speech or vice-versa. These other Englishes may lack prestige in England, but that reflects social circumstances. Linguistically speaking they cannot be regarded as defective languages: they are just different. To interpret their difference as defect is to miss the point.

167

5

The connection between accent and social class is another topic about which most of us have good intuitive knowledge and reasonably clear ideas. There are working-class accents and middle-class accents, and some people have quite irrational prejudices against one or the other: that is as far as our folk-linguistic takes us. But can we say on solid evidence that accent is related to class in any systematic way? To put it another way, how can we escape the circular situation of holding that accent is a cause of class differences which are in turn a cause of accent ones? So far as this country is concerned, the strict answer has to be No: the necessary research has not been done. If it had, it would have taken a representative cross-section of the population of a particular area, and would have investigated how each person in the sample talked in a variety of speech situations. The one major study in this area was done in New York City by Labov. Most of his findings seem to have a remarkably close 'fit' with many British cities, and they are summarised somewhat fully here because they are not accessible elsewhere.

What Labov did was to focus on a small area of New York City which was already very thoroughly researched by a team of sociologists. The Lower East Side is a mixed, mainly working-class district. He selected nearly 200 people as a representative sample of the social classes and groups in the district as a whole. Interviewing each of them individually, he ran the sessions so that they engaged in a range of language activities. These included casual chat, reminiscence, reading a passage aloud, and reading a word-list aloud. The whole interviews were tape-recorded, and were so constructed that the language of each subject included a number of key phonemes. For example, *bird* and *floor* include a sound belonging to the /r/ phoneme; another was the vowel in *pass*, *dance*, and *bad*; a third was the vowel in *caught*, *dog*, and *all*.

Labov's central discovery was not simply that members of different social classes spoke these sounds in different ways, but that the differences related regularly and systematically to social class. At the same time, the speech-sounds showed consistent variations, within any given class, according to the formality of the speech-activity being undertaken. Thus far we can say that Labov's findings confirm many people's intuitions about these matters. But Labov also investigated his informants' attitudes to the speech of people at various points in the social scale; what they thought about their own speech—its position in relation to other speakers, and its correctness or otherwise; and their view of the reputation of New York City speech outside the city. Most of his conclusions probably hold good for the language of many urban communities in the English-speaking world, although the details may vary from place to place. In listing these conclusions here, the examples given are taken from English situations.

1. People of all social groups usually have a very *in*accurate idea of how they speak themselves: lower middle-class people believed their own speech to be higher in the social scale than they judged speech of others which was phonetically identical to their own.

2. Particular forms of the key sounds are consistently regarded as high in prestige, and other forms as low. The English belief that certain kinds of 'dropped g's or h's' are 'low class' is a case in point.

3. These patterns of high and low prestige were the same for all the informants studied. This means the prestige of a particular accent is not just a matter of individual opinion: virtually all individuals have the same set of opinions.

4. The social classes at each end of the social scale show much less concern about the correctness of their own speech than those in the middle. What would in England be called the lower middle classes tend to copy what they regard as prestige sounds, just as they tend to be the most anxious parents who worry about the 'bad speech' their children pick up at school.

5. Women show much more of this 'linguistic anxiety' than men. This fits with the common experience, that worrying about little Johnnie's accent more often comes from Mum than from Father.

6. Many middle-class speakers show a conscious desire to lose any regional identity in their speech, and the resulting copying of prestige forms continues well into middle age.

7. New Yorkers rate the speech of their city as having much lower

169

prestige than did the outsiders who were asked for their views of it. In the same way, Birmingham people, if they are at all anxious about their speech, tend to regard a Birmingham accent as a stigma.

Some of Labov's most interesting findings are about the way speech sounds change in response to changes in the social setting. The more formal the speech activity involved, the more marked is the tendency to copy prestige sounds. Several informants related episodes where their daily work brought them into contact with people of different classes, and where this pattern could be heard. For example, an advertising agent told how he ended a visit to a working-class client by saying, inadvertently, "Thank you". On getting a good-humoured rebuke for being stuffy, he substituted a local, informal expression which was taken as more suitably friendly. To Labov, who was listening for the sounds employed, it was also one which used low-prestige sounds. Many of his informants relate instances of a quite unselfconscious switching from one level of formality to another. What they relate as differences in the words and phrases used provide evidence to the researcher of consistent differences in the speech-sounds involved.

New York City is clearly not the only place where moving away from prestige sounds is an effective gesture of friendliness. The phonetic details of Labov's work suggest, however, that it is no easier to do this deliberately and self-consciously than it is in England. But in both places a speech-form which uses prestige sounds in informal social situations is liable to be understood by some hearers as a sign of keeping one's hearers at a distance.

Finally, Labov points out clear signs of the tendency of some linguistically anxious speakers to over-compensate in their seeking after prestige sounds. This tendency, to what is technically known as hypercorrection, has been known in connection with usage for some years. What Labov does is to fill out the picture by showing how speech-sounds exhibit the same tendency. The over-anxious speaker who says things like "It is I" or "I do not know to whom you refer" is also likely to try to imitate the speech-sounds of RP, and to do it with a slight but telling inaccuracy. The writing of Fowler and Gowers, and of several other prescriptive manuals of English usage, at some points refer to the tendency to hypercorrection, but a principal effect of their work has been a very great increase in linguistic

170

anxiety in many of their readers. The sterile prescriptivism which supposes all language use to be of one kind, i.e. 'correct', has a limited place for limited uses, but as a set of linguistic tablets of the law most such manuals mislead by oversimplification.

6

Formality of utterance, then, appears in the *range* of sounds which a speaker can use. This creates the paradox that even the most 'correct 'speakers can easily be shown to be much less correct than they may suppose, especially in less formal situations. Obviously, the more formal a speaker's situation and utterance, the more closely will his sounds match his idea of prestige sounds. But as we have seen, most of us are rather bad judges of speech-sounds, especially our own. So one man's *range* of sounds may be quite different from another man's, without either of them realising it. Very few speakers in fact make use of the full range of variation which a study like Labov's can discover.

One consequence of this is that what is the least formal set of sounds in one speaker may sound to some other speakers more formal than anything they ever utter themselves. If you are an RP speaker, for example, no matter how informal and relaxed your speech becomes, you may still be regarded as too posh and too formal by many working-class people. The same would apply the other way round. Some working-class speakers may well be unable to encompass a degree of formality in their utterance which makes it acceptable to RP-speakers. The possibilities of misunderstanding inherent in this situation are obvious.

At this point we can refer back to the role of schemata, the patterns of interpretation which we impose on experience. These operate in the domain of speech-sounds as much as in any other area of experience. Each of us is in effect programmed to hear a speaker using a particular accent, which we recognise almost as soon as he begins speaking. Once we have responded to the cues which tell us we are listening to a Scot, for example, we automatically and imme-diately make all sorts of adjustments to what we are hearing, so that understanding it becomes easier. One way to test this out is to find a skilled accent-mimic, ask him to make up a talk in which he switches from one accent to another at intervals of, say, two sentences, and have this talk tried out on an audience which is not expecting anything like it. For many hearers the incongruity of what they hear will generate laughter, but for many others the result will be a deepening puzzlement. The extent to which our schemata programme us to hear RP as RP, and indeed English as English, can in turn be exploited: the politician who wishes to be accepted by the mass of voters is often careful to use speech-sounds which avoid prestige forms. This is a very difficult effect to achieve with precision, because we are not good judges of our own speech, and the difference between accurate mimicry and the tellingly inaccurate can be phonetically very small.

The practices of politicians, however, are only a public version of language uses which most people use some time or another. We have seen a number of instances of the fact that language varies in its formality. This is only possible because language-users are very sensitive to changes in the formality of the language they hear and speak. Labov's findings in this respect fit in very well with other treatments of formality, one of the most interesting being Joos's *The Five Clocks*. (There is a more complex, and perhaps technically more subtle treatment in Leech's *English in Advertising*, Chapter 8.) Joos regards spoken and written language as a continuum, and deals with both, but his account is included here because it parallels some aspects of Labov's work.

Joos suggests that the way we actually talk and write falls into five levels of formality. He labels these as Intimate, Casual, Consultative, Formal and Frozen. Intimate style very rarely gets into writing, but any very well-established social group will use it when there are no strangers about—married couples, games teams, work-mates in small groups. It is characterised by extreme reliance on the hearer knowing the whole context of an utterance. A husband who finds a note "11.30 perm." knows that his wife's hairdo takes $1\frac{1}{2}$ hours, and costs a known sum—so that she need only say where she is going in order to tell him how long she will be and how small is the danger of her staying on for bingo. Its other feature is a tendency to strip every utterance of every superfluous feature, giving it a clipped quality that makes the outsider despair of getting the hang of it—as, for instance, with technical exchanges between astronauts and base.

Consultative style is the middle, the medium, the norm of amicable

172

relations between colleagues and acquaintances. Between it and Intimate lies Casual, which we move into if we want to be friendly or to show we have no hostile feelings. The defining features of Consultative are that the addressee participates all the time and the speaker supplies information which he cannot just assume his hearer will know. Casual style, by comparison, assumes the other man knows the background information, and assumes the other man is participating without waiting for him to show it by 'I see' and 'Yes' and so on. Casual style, as Joos puts it "is for friends, insiders: addressed to a stranger, it serves to make him an insider simply by treating him as an insider." Casual style is more elliptical than Consultative, and its use of 'in' phrases has the effect of signalling to a hearer "Not everyone would understand what I'm saying, of course, but you do . . ."

On the other side of the spectrum, Consultative moves towards Formal when the regular and frequent participation of the hearer drops out—by reason of the size of the group, or the status differences in it, or uncertainty on either side as between strangers. A user of formal style dominates his immediate situation: it is just because participation by others makes for consultative that it is difficult not to be Formal (in language if not in manner) in a classroom. Formal language in this sense tends also to be more planned than Consultative: the chopping and changing, false starts, digressions, bracketings, and clarifications of Consultative are felt to be intolerable in Formal. But Formal remains a style which is possible in spoken language as well as written, because it can still make very full use of intonation. Indeed, where it is expository, and the connections between different parts of discourse are important for understanding, the intonation will reinforce these connections all the time.

But there are many uses of language which cannot depend on intonation to clarify or support meanings, and the meanings have to be spelled out, made explicit at every point. This is what Joos means by Frozen style. Because the hearer/reader cannot participate or question, Frozen text has to do its job particularly well. As Joos observes, "From the surpassing excellence of good frozen style, our folklore has derived the mistaken theory that is the ideal of all language." Most frozen text is, of course, written, but any lecture or address to a big or non-responding audience will also be in frozen style.

Joos makes the important point that these differences are primarily differences in the social relationships between people:

> "Good intimate style fuses two personalities. Good casual style integrates disparate personalities into a social group ... Good consultative style produces co-operation without the integration ... Good formal style informs the individual separately ... Good frozen style ... lures him into educating himself, so that he may the more confidently act what role he chooses."

But in the case of the last style, the text has one immense advantage over the other four: it can be re-inspected—that is, re-read at once, or thought over at a distance. This sets up a challenge to the writer to give his text the layers of meaning that re-inspection can uncover.

The relationship between Joos's five styles and Labov's various levels of formality in speech-sound is not immediate or direct. They approach the same general area from different standpoints. But it is clear enough that most native speakers of English will vary their style according to the social situations they are in. Obviously, many of these variations will show up in speech-sounds (if we care to listen for them) as well as in more obvious ways.

Are we to conclude that the different levels of formality are of equal value? Well, are we to conclude that the different social relationships which give rise to them are of anything *but* equal value? Our folk-linguistic maintains a peculiarly rigid set of equations about this: it tells us that the formal equals the correct, and the informal equals the incorrect. A solicitor recently found that his new secretary couldn't spell *acknowledge*, so he used *receive*, and when she couldn't spell that either he said *have read* ... In the upshot his partners took exception, not to the girl's deficiencies, but to their colleague's skill in circumventing them. This was because his strategy forced him out of "Our Mr. Swindon begs to acknowledge ..." into "I have read ...", and poor Mr. Swindon's legal colleagues believed that only the formality of the third person was 'correct'. This is but one more example of that connection between status, social control, and the expression of values discussed in Chapter 6. In all seriousness, though, one must ask what the ordinary clients of such firms must feel. Is their sense of being unable to keep up with such habits a constructive contribution to society? Are they not reduced to the kind of apprehension which

174

makes the schoolboy inarticulate before his teacher and the office junior silent before his employer? Such people go running for the nearest boy who can handle the language of these extraordinary beings, or for the manuals of good usage which, sadly, only seem to deepen their predicament.

What then should be the role of school and teacher? Surely it must first of all be to recognise variety in spoken language, to discriminate between the casual style of chatter among friends and the consultative style of discussion about cylinder heads. And the school needs somehow to convey this discrimination. Most of its pupils will have a strong intuitive awareness of much in this chapter, and these intuitions can be turned to good account—if the school and the teacher can resist the urge to diminish ways of speaking they do not use themselves. The gift of language in a normal child is never so small as to justify the disparagement it often receives from teachers. The disparagement of natural speech which goes on in many classrooms and homes damages the only foundation that many children have for the development of competence. It is also a strong enough force in our society to justify a policy of seeking to restore the 'linguistic morale' of whole classes. This in turn may mean making them conscious of just how much they intuitively know, making them aware of just how much more they can come to know by attention and by listening. The explorations into language that follow from treating formality as a range rather than a crude contrast of good and bad can be of great value in such a policy.

FURTHER READING

D. Abercrombie, *Studies in Phonetics and Linguistics* (Language and Language Learning Series, Oxford).

C. Hannam, P. Smyth and N. Stephenson, *Young teachers and reluctant learners* (Penguin).

D. H. Hargreaves, *Social Relations in the Secondary School* (Routledge).

B. Jackson and D. Marsden, *Education and the Working Class* (Penguin).

M. Joos, *The Five Clocks* (Harcourt Brace).

N. Keddie, "The Social Basis of Classroom Knowledge" in *Knowledge and Control*, ed. M. Young (Collier Macmillan).

W. Labov, *The Social Stratification of English in New York City* (Centre for Applied Linguistics, Washington D.C.).

W. Labov, "Some Phonological Correlates of Social Stratification" in *The Ethnography of Communication*, ed. J. J. Gumperz and D. Hymes.

R. Lacey, *Hightown Grammar* (Manchester U.P.).

J. J. Pearce, *Some Linguistic Aspects of English Language Examinations* (Papers in Linguistics and English Teaching, Series II, Longman).

D. Pidgeon, *Teacher Expectation and Pupil Performance* (National Foundation for Education Research).

F. Williams (ed.), *Language and Poverty* (Chicago, Markham Publishing Co.).

Eleven   Diversity in written English

1

For most people written English is just written English, good, bad or indifferent. Our folk-linguistic tells us that there is a norm of Good Plain Prose, and we are writing reasonably well if we come up to that standard, and badly if we do not. This belief has a close relative in the feeling that whatever we write will be Good if it manages without being technical and Bad if it does not—the sense that, well, some people have to write as specialists for specialists, but that's their business, and so long as they don't publicise their sin we can put up with it. This is the linguistic equivalent of the old notion of the Gentleman-amateur, the idea that an educated person doesn't dirty his hands with anything technical. But there is a quite different piece of folk-linguistic which tells us that the better a writer is, the more distinctive his style is: that is, the Best Writers are somehow free from the obligation to write Good Plain English, and are allowed to be Different. These two beliefs are, of course, mutually contradictory. The former has been explored in Peter Doughty's *Current Attitudes to Written English*. In effect, Good Plain Prose is a notion which cannot be made to fit any existing linguistic facts. It is rather like that elusive gentleman, the General Reader: very convenient for describing a large group of people, but a bad description of any particular individual—no reader, as Ross of *The New Yorker* said, is ever general.

So written language consists of texts written for particular readers by particular writers in particular situations. Its range is daunting, even within the scope of what Joos called Frozen Style. Linguists have made a number of forays into this field, seeking to define through detailed analytical description what it is that distinguishes one writer from another, one genre from another, and so on. This is the least developed area of the linguistic sciences, and follows the basic procedure of linguistics by taking the *text* as its field of inspection. Here we take a set of examples of written language and look at the *situations* in which their language comes to be used, the audiences to whom they are addressed, and the degree to which they use technical language.

177

2

Consider the following:

A. Once upon a time in Spain there was a little bull and his name was Ferdinand. All the other little bulls he lived with would run and jump and butt their heads together, but not Ferdinand. He liked to sit just quietly and smell the flowers. He had a favourite spot out in the pasture under a cork-tree. It was his favourite tree and he would sit in its shade all day and smell the flowers.

B. Navy wool crêpe, opposite, and cream suede ribbons for the binding; wrapover skirt, simple open waistcoat. By Baccarat, £38, at Harvey Nichols, Matching navy cashmere sweater, by Pringle, about £11, Hills' Cashmere House, Bond St. Gold neck chain with lock and key, silver bracelet, crocodile strapped watch, all from Cartier.

C. The work is of a basic nature, with some University contacts, but is directly applicable to company products, and will initially involve a range of interesting problems concerning the chrystalline morphology and rheological properties of low friction polymers.

D. With the switch mechanism removed, the unit can be connected in accordance with the diagram shown on p. 5. The four-way terminal block provides separate connections for the synchronous motor, but if this is not required a light current link should be inserted between terminals 3 and 4, with the neutral taken to terminal 2, as shown in the alternative wiring arrangement. The extended cable cover (3) providing conduit entry is fitted by sliding it onto the dovetails moulding on the case and extending the locking tab (4) and securing it with the screw located inside the case.

E. A void marriage is one that will be regarded by every court in any case in which the existence of the marriage is in issue as never having taken place and can be so treated by both parties to it without the necessity of any decree annulling it: a voidable marriage is one that will be regarded by every court as a valid subsisting marriage until a decree annulling it has been pronounced by a court of competent jurisdiction.

F. (a) The interpretation of physical and human patterns as shown on Ordnance Survey maps and plans, and on air photographs studied in conjunction with these. The practice of the geographer's techniques, such as interpreting views and recording them by field sketching, making and interpreting selective tracings from topographical maps, drawing transect diagrams in the field and from maps, constructing and interpreting block diagrams, construction and interpreting cross-sections and long profiles.

The most obvious difference between the six examples is quite simply the job each text is trying to do. One is telling a story, while the second is a caption for a fashion photograph. The third is seeking to recruit applicants for a specific job without getting too many totally unsuitable replies. The fourth is part of the wiring instructions for a time-switch, while the fifth is part of a legal judgement in the Court of Appeal, and the last is a specification or list of items of work to be done. These differences are differences according to *use*, and they account for some, but not all, of the particular characteristics of each. 'Telling a story' implies a serial ordering of events. Nothing is taken as read or already known from outside the bounds of the story. Passage B, by contrast, is located very firmly in the context of the fashion-magazine pages for which it is written. The Sunday newspaper advertisement for a senior scientist (Passage C) is fairly specific about what kind of scientific work is involved: the research is 'basic' but not 'pure'—the scientist whose aim is narrowly academic is therefore put off, while the practical research worker is given precise guidance about what he is in for if he applies.

Passage D is very different again: like B, it is written to be read in immediate conjunction with something outside the text, in this case a Venner time-switch of the sort used to control a street light or a central heating system. But between the physical object and the text quoted there also lies a diagram, on which various parts of the object are identified by numbers. The language here has a job to do which is so specific that its efficiency, considered simply as language, can be tested. In fact, a number of brands of time-switch were given to a group of apprentices finishing their training as electrical fitters, and they were asked to make mock-up wirings according to the printed instructions, working in groups of three in a technical college class. This text was the only one which managed completely to forestall

179

mistakes in the wiring, so proving efficient in this strict sense.

Passage D makes little sense, of course, without the diagram and the mechanism it refers to. But this dependence upon context applies in varying degrees to *all* the texts cited. B requires the photographs it describes, and is careful to supply only the additional information that the photographs themselves cannot convey: one would judge from the text, quote correctly, that the photographs in question were in black and white. Passage E is dependent on context to a similar degree but in a different way, and its particular use of language cannot be fully understood without a knowledge of the context. It is a part of a legal judgement handed down in 1948 by the then Master of the Rolls, on a point of law which is of some importance to divorce lawyers and their clients. What it seems to be saying is that you cannot seek a divorce if your 'marriage' is, in legal respects, not a proper marriage at all: the law cannot try to void that which is void by definition. But the context of this judgement is a long history of legal decisions in which the precise application of the distinction between a void and a voidable marriage had been a little uncertain. This judgement seeks to be exhaustive in that respect, and so every particle of the text has some force. Thus, 'by every court' and 'in any case' are part of the exhaustive definition, and are quite different in meaning from the colloquial use of 'in any case'. The absence of commas in this passage is also intentional, since a bit of text placed between commas can become a cause of argument in court about whether it refers to the word immediately before the first comma or whether it has a wider reference. The absence of commas is saying, in effect, that a void marriage is defined as having characteristics x, y and z, and *all* such characteristics have to be present without qualification.

Passage F could be criticised on the same ground as Passage B for being 'not in sentences'. It is like this because of its use: here language is being used to make a specification, a detailed, specific list of items. Where the items are of work in a programme of study, the specification is known as a syllabus. As we would expect in such a context, its most distinctive features have to do with the degree of technicality in the language as much as with the audience addressed or the use itself. Even Passage A depends on context: part of its point lies in it, since the illustrations show trees bearing *bunches* of corks.

180

3

Earlier chapters have stressed the nature of language as something involving interaction: the language-user is always a speaker/hearer or writer/reader. The use of written language makes it possible for the writing and the reading of one text to be widely separate in space and time, but the basic fact remains that any piece of writing is necessarily addressed to an audience. How the language is used will, in part, define that audience: if I do not know what 'rheological' means, Text C's use of that term defines its audience so as to exclude me, and if I am typical in this respect I probably will not mind very much. I may think I know something about the law, so that I am not put off by such phrases as 'annulled by a court of competent jurisdiction'. If I am typical, I might well not understand at first glance just why so much fuss is being made over a tiny distinction like that between *void* and *voidable*. Again, I might well follow the first half of F quite readily, but would jib at 'transect diagrams'. Our readiness to be put off by a piece of written language is often a reflection not so much of the language used, as of our own knowledge and experience. Ths fact bears closely on the idea of a reader as an audience, and works both ways: a text may mean very much more to its intended audience than others would imagine possible.

For example, the intended audience for B is one which will know that Cartier is the name of a very expensive jeweller. 'Gold' in such a context is clearly the precious metal, not a colour, 'crocodile' is the reptile-skin and not an imitation. This readership will know too whether Baccarat is an exclusive sort of clothing shop. The placing of this kind of apparently bald statement of fact side by side with such other details as '£38' can mean relatively little to some audiences and a great deal to others. It may well be that at the time of this particular text, for example, £38 was an exceptionally high price for that particular firm or an exceptionally low one. The point is that a significant part of *Vogue*'s audience, being in the trade, will know the relevant facts. A more light-hearted case is Passage A, written as it is for an audience which can see the book's illustrations, and which may take the text as comment on the pictures rather than the other way about.

Use and audience are separate dimensions on which written language can vary, but are not necessarily independent of each other. We have seen that part of the use of language in Text C was precisely to define the advertisement's audience, positively and negatively. The precision of 'low friction polymers' and 'crystalline morphology' restricts the audience being addressed and this effect is part of the writer's purpose. Text D is quite different in this respect: the use or purpose is within a context which includes a defined audience. The only people ever likely to read the wiring instructions for a time-switch are people who have the job of installing time-switches. But such an audience is not as uniformly competent or skilled as writers of instructions of this sort may suppose. The electrician apprentices who used the instructions found much of this text superfluous, but pointed out that part of the superiority of this text to the others lay in its catering for the do-it-yourself installer: it leaves very little to the user's guesswork.

Passage E is addressed to a much more specialised audience: as the earlier comment on its punctuation suggests, it is written in the knowledge that it is likely to be referred to as authoritative, and its real audience is therefore both very limited in numbers and indefinitely extended in time. Only the law-student or lawyer, and the divorce-law specialist at that, is likely to have read it with any close attention. The writer can build in great density of meaning, and need make few concessions. A solicitor, writing to a lay client inquiring about the status of his marriage, will write quite differently, thus: "If your marriage is legal and valid as a marriage, court action is necessary to annul it. But if there is any reason to think that a court would regard your marriage as in a legal sense not a valid marriage, it's no good hoping for a divorce—because divorce only applies to valid marriages." A wise solicitor, of course, will also check that all the other elements in the ruling are looked into, without necessarily worrying his client over what will seem irrelevant details.

Passage E is, of course, very formal indeed. The certainty that it will be inspected for years to come by capable lawyers is a fact in the writer's situation which typifies what Joos means by Frozen style. This is the feature which it has in common with Passage F: as an examination syllabus, it too will be consulted by large numbers of specialists, and we shall look at the principal consequence of this in the next section. But in Joos's terms, Passage D is also Frozen, since

182

it has to stand up to repeated inspection by diverse readers. Passages B and C are both transitory: when the job is filled or the fashions change no one will have the slightest interest in the language of either. For that reason, if no other, we could describe C as Formal rather than Frozen. Whether B is labelled Formal or Consultative is probably a matter of opinion, but the use of the 'colloquial' surface in B does not of itself point to Casual style. A, however, is more subtle: it is, after all, written for publication as a piece of children's literature, to be read aloud to young children by adults whose ability to see more in a text than the children must in some measure be taken into account. The apparent simplicity of the sentences is not associated with the audience (of children), if only because we have to recognise even simpler structures in the short stories of Hemingway. But the text is carefully wrought, and that is sufficient to classify it as Frozen so far as its style is concerned.

4

An element in our folk-linguistic is the pressure which many writers feel, and many readers exert, for a text to avoid being technical. It is possible now to look at this question again, by asking which of these six passages is the most technical in its use of language. There is no linguistic answer to this question. Certain features of the texts bear on it, but they will not take us very far. The technical terms in C have already been referred to, and if we take 'technical' to mean 'defining the audience narrowly' this passage would come high on the list—but the same would hold for Passage E. Passage D uses a number of technical terms, such as *four-way terminal block, light current link, conduit entry, synchronous motor*. This set of *terms*, like those in the scientist advertisement, and unlike the language of the legal judgement, is not accessible to the reader from the immediate context: the amount of prior knowledge assumed in the reader is considerable. In this sense of 'assuming prior knowledge' it could be held that the caption from *Vogue* is just as technical as the legal judgement: every reader is assumed to know what is a *wrapover skirt* or the nature of *cashmere*. A certain technicality of language use is thus a natural and even necessary part of all our language behaviour, whether we are in a cycle shop asking for a *valve-insert*, in the radio shop asking for a spare *sapphire stylus*, or at the ironmonger's seeking a *non-caustic* oven cleaner.

One of the difficulties with technical language is that there is overlap between technical and non-technical contexts, and the same stock of words often has to do duty in both. Passage F is a good example of this. There are some obvious technical terms in it, but some others are not so readily identified. *Transect diagrams* and *long profiles* are obviously technical to the geography field, and a *selective tracing* is likely to be rather different here from one in engineering drawing. More subtly, *construct* is a rigidly defined term in elementary geometry, and is as tightly defined, i.e. technical, here. Much the same holds for *interpret*: geography as a discipline has a defining tradition of what constitutes interpretation in this field and at this level. It is hard to see how the examiners could write an A Level Geography syllabus without using technical language in this way. The effect of using it must be, in some cases at least, to define some potential readers as outside the intended audience. Where the language has a technical job to do, as here, this is always understood and acceptable. The difficulty arises, and the complaints begin, when the language has a technical job to do on a topic which most laymen, often wrongly, believe to be a non-technical one. Use of technical language in such a context is liable to make many readers complain that what they had thought of as eminently simple is being made unnecessarily complicated—that is, they object to what they see as jargon.

Darwin's *Origin of Species* received not a few favourable critical reviews, in spite of the storm aroused in some quarters at the time of its publication, but even some of the most favourable objected to its jargon. At that time, the tradition of gentleman-amateur was still very much alive in the biological sciences, and Darwin's professionalism annoyed such people. Something rather similar seems to hold in the social sciences today. For example, a sentence in a long and technical paper was recently mocked by a journalist as fatuously obvious. "Passage of time between learning and recall is the critical defining variable for forgetting." The journalist complained bitterly at the waste of money in financing such platitudes. In its context the sentence is far from fatuous: the findings of experimental psychology about learning, forgetting, and recall, as defined by the specialised test conditions of laboratories, have presented many puzzles about which variable was the most important for each process. The journalist had missed, or ignored, the fact that in this context such common-language words as *memory* and *forgetting* are used as technical terms with restricted meanings. Another instance is the

184

well-known entry under *Jargon* in Fowler's *Modern English Usage*, which berated sociology for using its own technical language—implying that it had no right to one.

Specialists can be forgiven for feeling that laymen seem to want it both ways—objecting to anything technical as jargon, and deriding anything expressed in non-technical language as platitudinous. There is a streak of the linguistic Luddite in most of us: we tend to reject or criticise every other man's technical language as jargon. One of the difficulties is that language users are apt to be unaware of when they are being technical. But the use of technical language in writing is at bottom socially determined, by the kind of interaction between reader and writer that we either want to set up or have to hope for. The social groups we address in writing have expectations about the written language likely to be addressed to them, and one aspect of competence is to know something about these groups and their expectations.

5

The foregoing sections have stressed that the most obvious ways in which written language can vary are reflections of social patterns. The purpose of this last section is to relate this emphasis to the treatment of variety which is already established in linguistic studies and has become quite well known among teachers. How does this social view of diversity relate to such ideas as Register or other treatments of variety?

Register is a useful term for pointing to the lines along which particular texts can vary. It makes use of three major types of difference between them: Field, Mode and Tenor. Field refers to the institutional setting in which a piece of language occurs, and embraces not only the subject-matter in hand but the whole activity of the speaker as a participant in a setting. The Field of Passage B, above, would thus be defined as 'fashion-plate caption in high grade fashion magazine'—and the subject-matter of the text enters little into this.

Mode refers to the channel of communication adopted: not only the choice between spoken and written medium, but much more detailed choices can be described under this head. Passage A could thus be described as written, but written to be read aloud. Such distinctions as those between text written to be read, text written to be read aloud, and text written to be read aloud as if newly received (e.g. in a letter which arrives in the action of a play), would be distinctions under Mode—to the extent that these differences can be related to formal differences in the language used.

Tenor or Style refers to the relationship between participants and the variations in style which reflect these relations. Tenor embraces not merely variation in formality, such as Joos deals with, but deals with such questions as the permanence or otherwise of the relationship and the degree of emotional charge in it.

Another scheme, put forward by Crystal and Davy in *Interpreting English Style*, offers no less than ten categories into which the linguistic features of texts may be classified. The description of the linguistic details of specific texts becomes in this way a more elaborate business—for those who want that sort of thing. But the great majority of pupils and students do not need to be able to make use of so complex a system of explicit linguistic description. We can encourage a great deal of useful observation and understanding, however, simply by looking at the varieties of written language in terms of use, audience, and technicality, without asking for a technical analysis of register.

This chapter has suggested that in looking at written texts and in trying to write them, it may often be useful, especially with older students, to have certain criteria available for the discussion of language which are both an advance on those of our folk-linguistic and short of the full technicality of linguistics. From the point of view of the secondary student, we can sum this up by suggesting that language in use always involves a *context* of languaging, a *message* to convey, a *role* in which to convey it, and an *audience* to be addressed. The student who is asked to speak or write is always likely to do a better job if he is clear about all four of these factors. This in turn may call for a greater degree of explicitness about them than some teachers are accustomed to. Thus, the term 'essay' does not specify a context with enough clarity for many pupils. The ways in which composition tasks are set in schools need to be more specific about the message-content being invited. One of the striking contrasts in Use of English examinations has been between the success of questions which specified a role in which the candidate was required to write, and the relative failure of questions which were not specific about this. The instance of examinations reminds us of the problem, evident to many examiners, that candidates often show great uncertainty about the kind of audience they are addressing in their answers.

FURTHER READING

D. Crystal and D. Davy, *Investigating English Style* (Longman).

A. Davies, "Some Problems in the Use of Language Varieties in Teaching" (Educational Review, Vol. 20, No. 2, 1968).

P. S. Doughty, *Current Attitudes to Written English*, Nuffield Papers in Linguistic and English Teaching (Longman).

N. E. Enkvist, J. Spencer and M. J. Gregory, *Linguistics and Style* (Language and Language Learning Series, Oxford).

M. A. K. Halliday, A. McIntosh and P. Strevens, *The Linguistic Sciences and Language Teaching*, Chapter 4 (Longman).

G. N. Leech, *English in Advertising*, especially Chapters 7–10 (Longman).

G. N. Leech, *A Linguistic Guide to English Poetry* (Longman).

Randolph Quirk, *The Use of English* (Longman).

APPENDIX

Relation of *Language in Use* units to chapters of
Exploring Language.

Chapter 2
  C4
  D1, 2, 3, 4, 5
  F8, 9, 10
  G8

Chapter 3
  C5
  D5

Chapter 4
  D7, 8
  E1, 2, 3, 5, 8, 9
  F1, 2, 3, 4
  H1, 2, 3, 7
  J2

Chapter 5
  H1, 2, 3, 4, 5, 9, 10
  J4
  K3, 4, 5

Chapter 6
  D13
  F6
  G11
  H7, 8
  J1, 3, 4
  K1, 2, 3, 4, 5

Chapter 7
  A1, 2, 3, 8
  B1
  C1, 8, 10
  D1, 6, 10, 11, 12
  E 5, 7
  G8, 9, 10
  J11
  K1, 2, 6, 7

Chapter 8
  C3, 4, 5, 6
  F9
  J4, 5, 6, 7, 8, 9

Chapter 9
  A7
  B4
  C1, 9, 10
  G10
  J11
  K11

Chapter 10
  B1, 3
  C3, 4, 6, 7
  F8, 9, 10, 11
  J6, 7

Chapter 11
  A2, 3, 4, 5
  F7
  G8, 9

Glossary

ACCENT
See Chapter Ten, passim.

AUDIENCE
The person (or persons) addressed by a speaker or writer. A person's use of language is strongly influenced by his notion of who he is speaking to, or writing to or for. See PARTICIPANT or SETTING.

CATEGORY
Human beings begin, from their earliest days to sort, or classify, their experience, so that their view of the world is built up from a vast number of individual entities which are classified into named categories. "This is done more or less automatically, continuously, and from our earliest days. The criteria we use consciously or unconsciously for classification vary with our purpose, that is, we select certain properties of a thing and ignore others, according to convenience; thus we may arrange books according to size, or colour, or author, or subject, or date of publication." (*The Anatomy of Judgement*—Abercrombie (Pelican), p. 133).

CODE
A system of symbols used as means of conveying information, as in Morse Code, colour coding, genetic code, etc. For Elaborated and Restricted Code, as Bernstein has used the terms, see Chapter Six, p. 104.

COMPETENCE
The ability of a speaker or writer to meet adequately the linguistic demands of a situation. See Chapter Seven passim.

CULTURE
The entire way of life of members of a community; what they habitually do; the network of values, attitudes and beliefs that gives a society, or part of a society, a recognisable identity.

DIALECT
See Chapter Ten, p. 160.

EXPRESSIVE
The way in which language conveys the views, attitudes and feelings of speaker or writer. See INFORMATION.

FOLK-LINGUISTIC
See Chapter One, p. 8.

FOLK-SOCIAL
See Chapter Five, pp. 62–3.

FORMALITY
The respect in which language varies according to the relationship between user and audience. Formality is a continuum from least formal to most formal, not a simple choice between formal and informal. Joos classifies this continuum into five broad ranges, which he calls intimate, casual, consultative, formal and frozen. For him, intimate style rarely occurs in written language, frozen style rarely in spoken. A three-fold division into casual, consultative and formal makes a useful beginning in the classroom. Joos's account is in *The Five Clocks* (Harcourt Brace); another account will be found in *English in Advertising*, Geoffrey Leech, (Longman).

INFORMATION
That which is conveyed by language other than the speaker's attitude and feeling. See EXPRESSIVE.

LANGUAGE
Common Language What the speaker of a language would ordinarily use; the meanings which words carry in everyday usage; language not used technically by a trade or profession, or in a particular discipline or branch of knowledge.

Model of Language The conceptions of language, what it is and how it works,

189

that the language user derives from his own experience of language. See, for example, M. A. K. Halliday's *Relevant Models of Language*, discussed in Chapter Three, p. 46.

Mother Tongue The language learnt initially in the environment in which one grows up.

Natural Language Language used in human communities (e.g. English, French, Korean) as contrasted with artificial language such as that constructed for programming computers.

Technical Language Language which is given a precisely definable meaning by its use in, and virtual restriction to, a particular field of intellectual enquiry, such as Literary Criticism or Bio-Chemistry; language which carries a meaning different from its common language meaning through its use in a particular professional, commercial or industrial activity; language which is fully meaningful only in a highly restricted context like a sailing dinghy or a work-bench because it relates to a specific set of operations.

LINGUISTIC REALITY
See Chapter One, p. 12.

LINGUISTIC RULE
The linguist's description of the way in which a specific aspect of language actually works, as opposed to prescriptions which purport to show how people ought to use it.

MARKED/UNMARKED
A widely occurring feature of human behaviour is the habit of linking together bits of experience and treating one member of such a pair as the one we usually expect to find. We thus have to use a special name for, or otherwise *mark*, the one we are not expecting. Nurses are expected to be female, numbers to be positive, girls to be unmarried. Otherwise, we say 'male nurse', place a minus sign in front of the number and put a ring on the girl's finger.

190

MESSAGE
Everything a speaker or writer intends to convey by his use of language. Its content as opposed to its form. See UTTERANCE.

PARTICIPANT
In a language SETTING (q.v.), a participant may be a Speaker or Hearer, and will usually be both at different times. A participant may have a marked effect on the language used even though silent himself. The relationship between Writer and Reader is also a participant relationship.

PHONEME
See Chapter Nine, p. 142.

PHONOLOGY
The systematic sound-patterns of a language, comprising its set of distinctive and mutually contrastive sounds, and the set of possible ways of combining them. See Chapter Nine, pp. 140–2.

REGISTER
See Chapter Eleven, Section 5.

RP
Abbreviation for Received Pronunciation. See Chapter Ten, Section 3.

SCHEMATA
See Chapter Four, pp. 51–2. See also CATEGORY.

SETTING
The context in which language is used, spoken and written. It is the various features of the setting, like the PARTICIPANTS and the location, which constrain the user's choice of language.

SOCIAL GROUPS
Individuals who come together for some purpose, whether professional, commercial, recreational, intellectual, or otherwise. Social groups may be temporary or persist over a long period of time. The persistence of a social group over any length of time brings about the development of particular ways of using language, which will

distinguish members of the groups from others, while giving cohesion and a sense of identity to the group itself.

SOCIAL REALITY
See Chapter One, p. 12.

SOCIAL TALK
Social talk covers the wide range of conversational gambits which people use, not merely to fill the silence, but to maintain a distance between them, to deal with interruptions.

STYLE
In linguistics, a term denoting 'level of formality'. See FORMALITY, and Chapter Ten, Section 6.

TERM
A word becomes a term when the particular distinction which it expresses is restricted to a particular field and essential for an understanding of the conceptual basis of that field. The entries in this glossary are, in this sense, terms.

UTTERANCE
The form which conveys the message. It can be spoken or written.

VARIETY
Language distinguished according to user (e.g. dialect) or use (e.g. the language of sermons).